Rural Missouri in the Fall

Scenic Photography
By Atwood Cutting

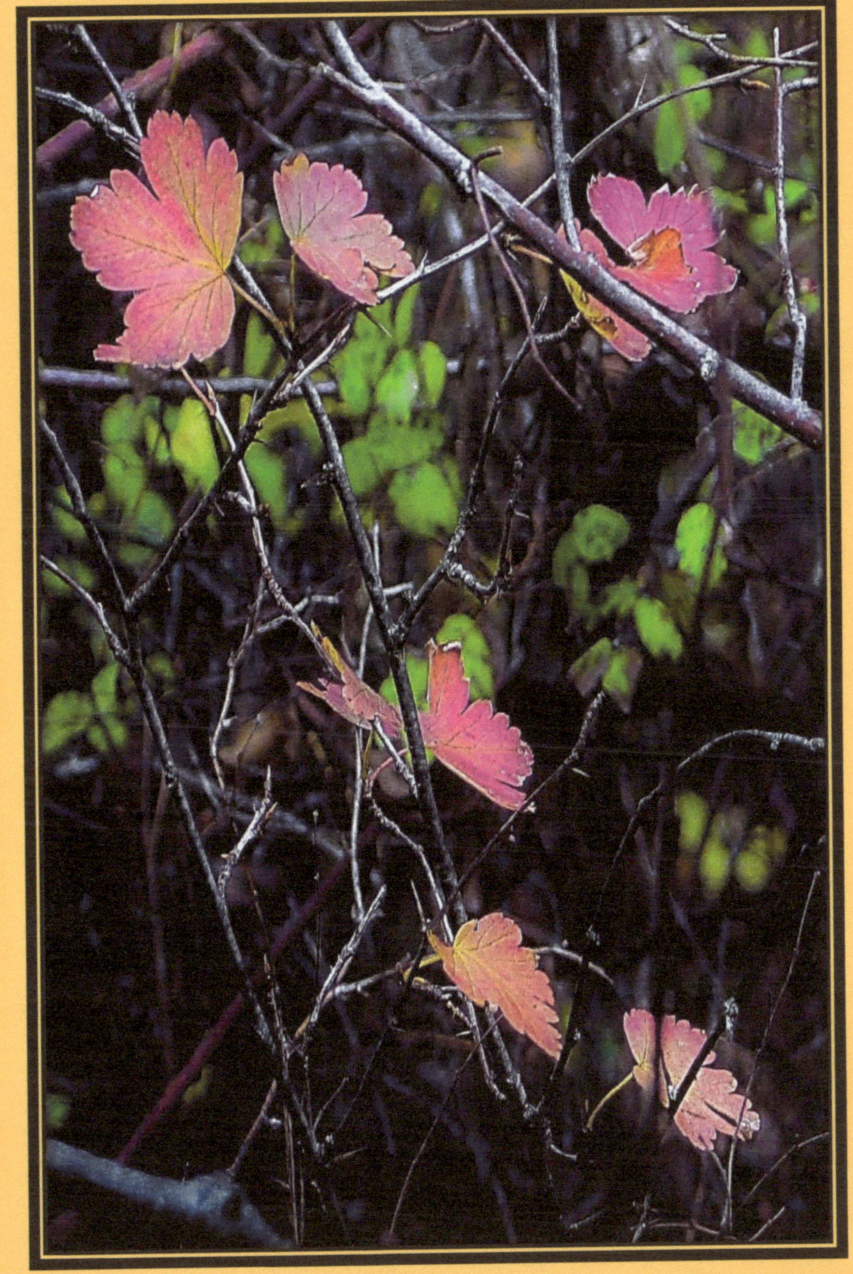

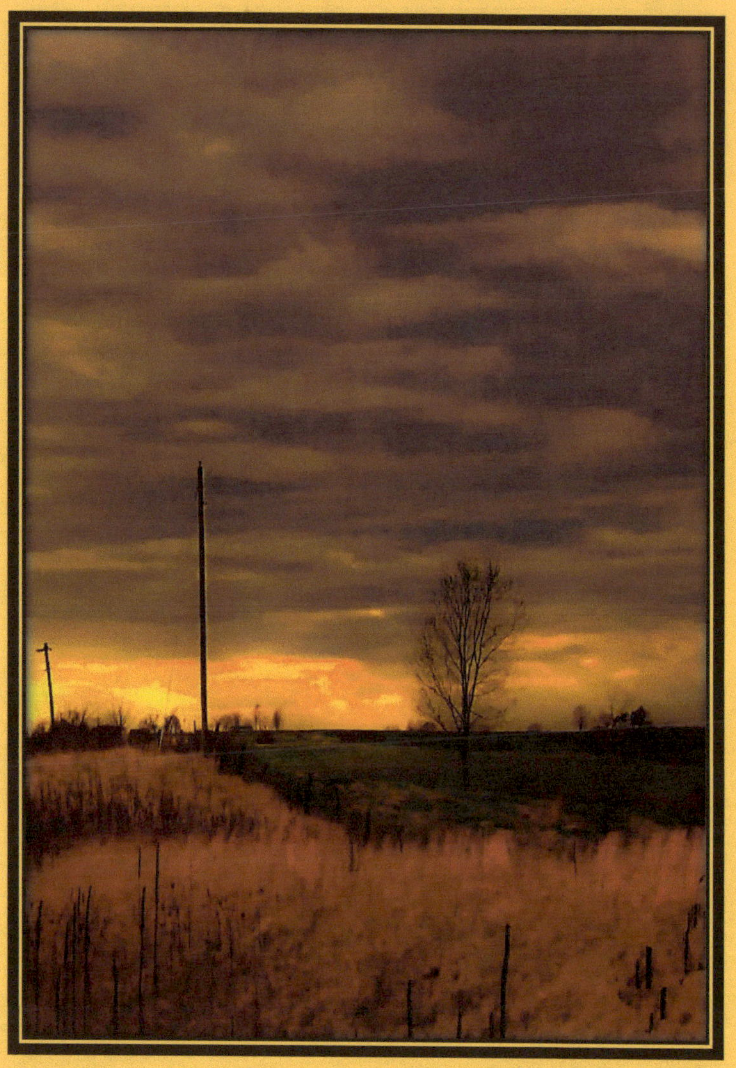

Rural Missouri in the Fall

Scenic Photography
By Atwood Cutting

Copyright 2019, Atwood Cutting
Echo Hill Arts Press, LLC

ISBN: 9780999506127

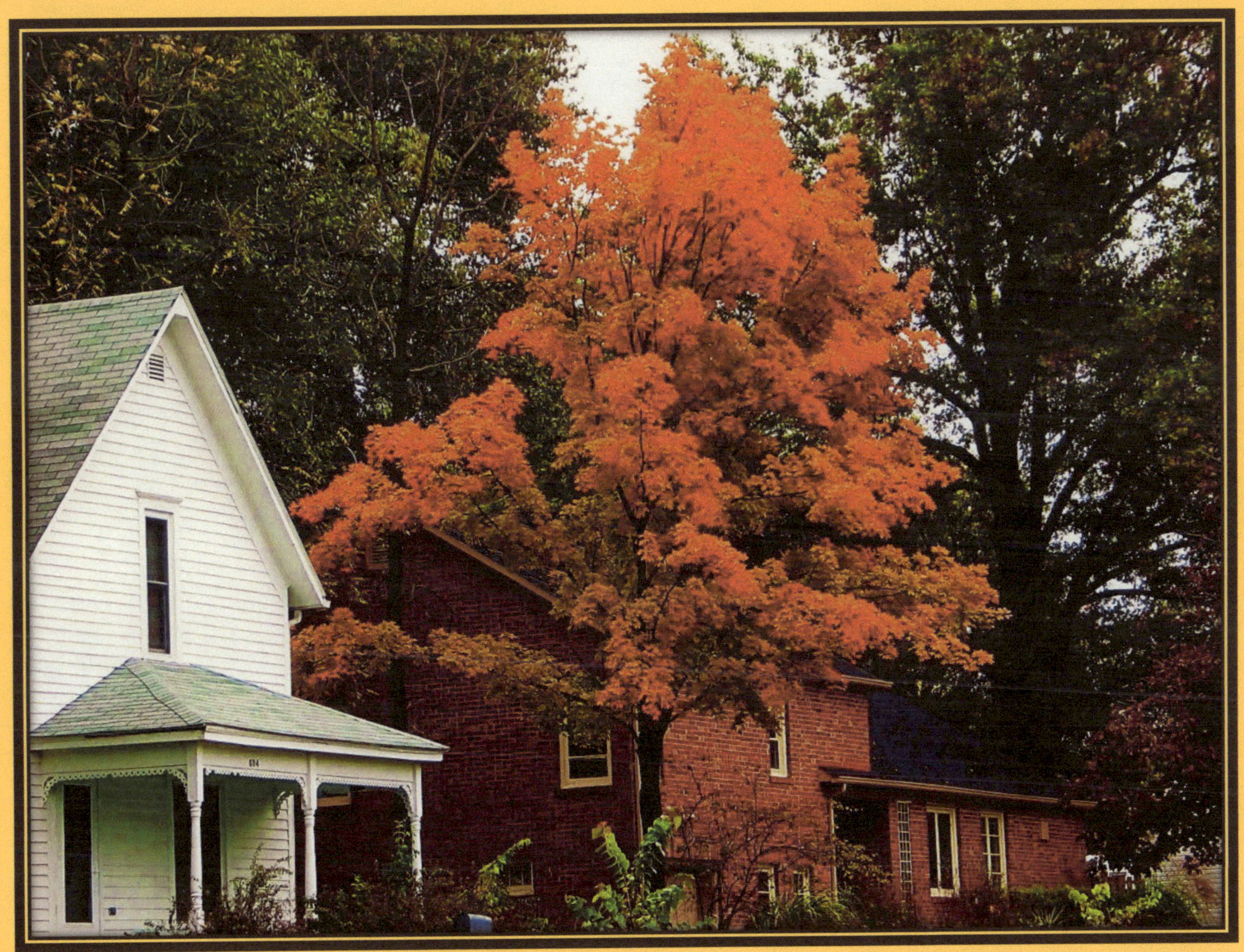

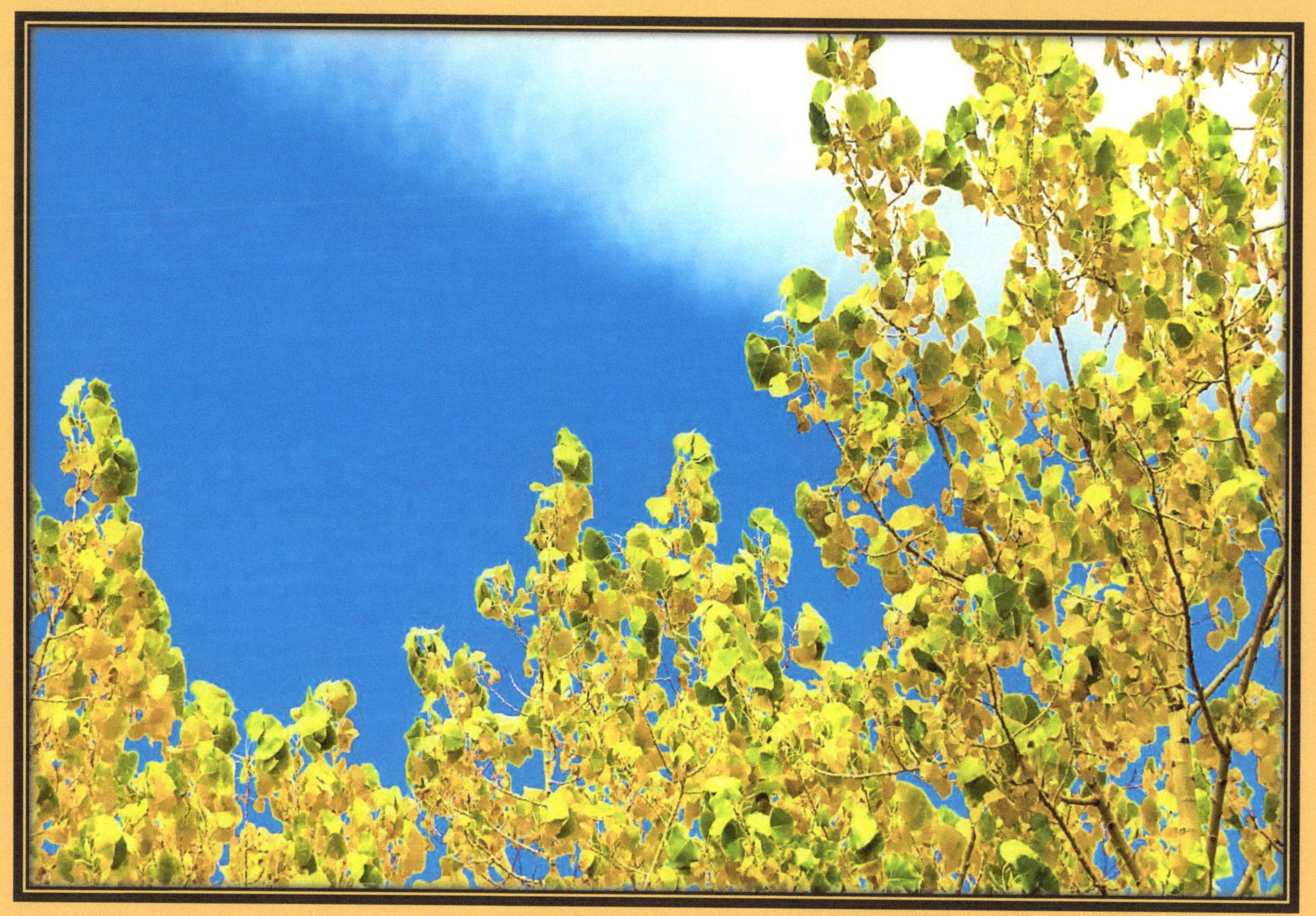

Missouri is full of fertile farmland.

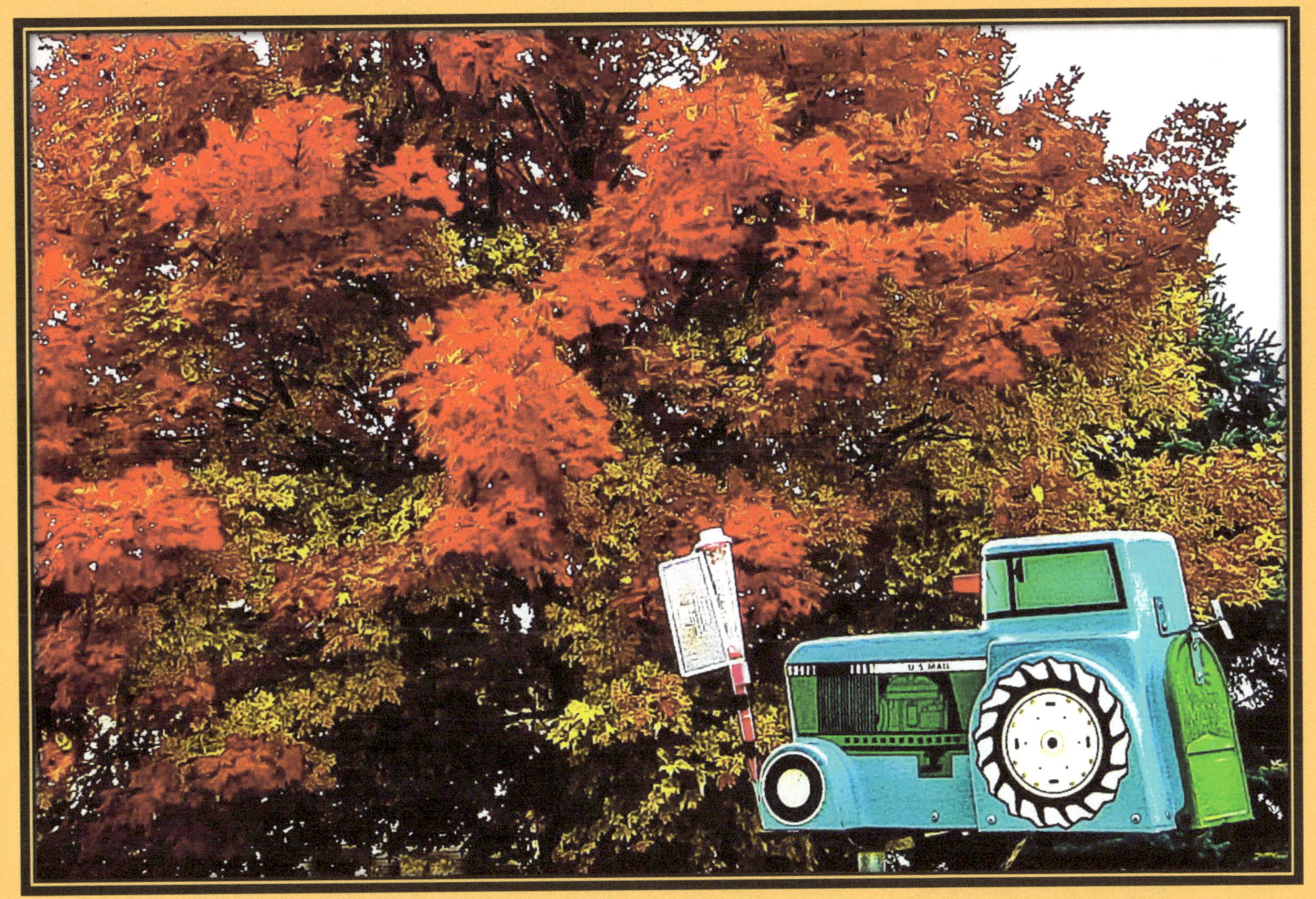

Trees luxuriate here
and wax brilliant in the fall.

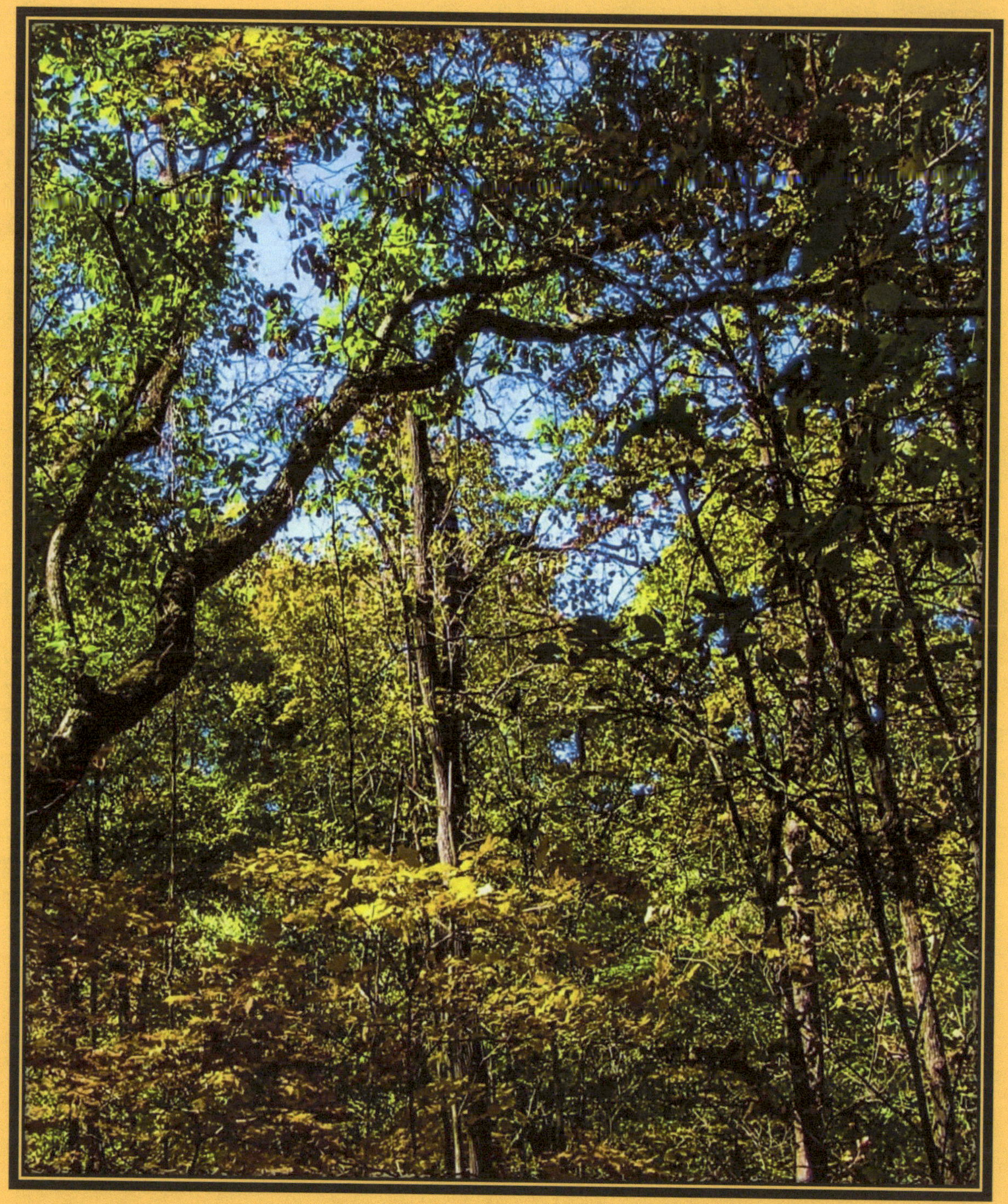

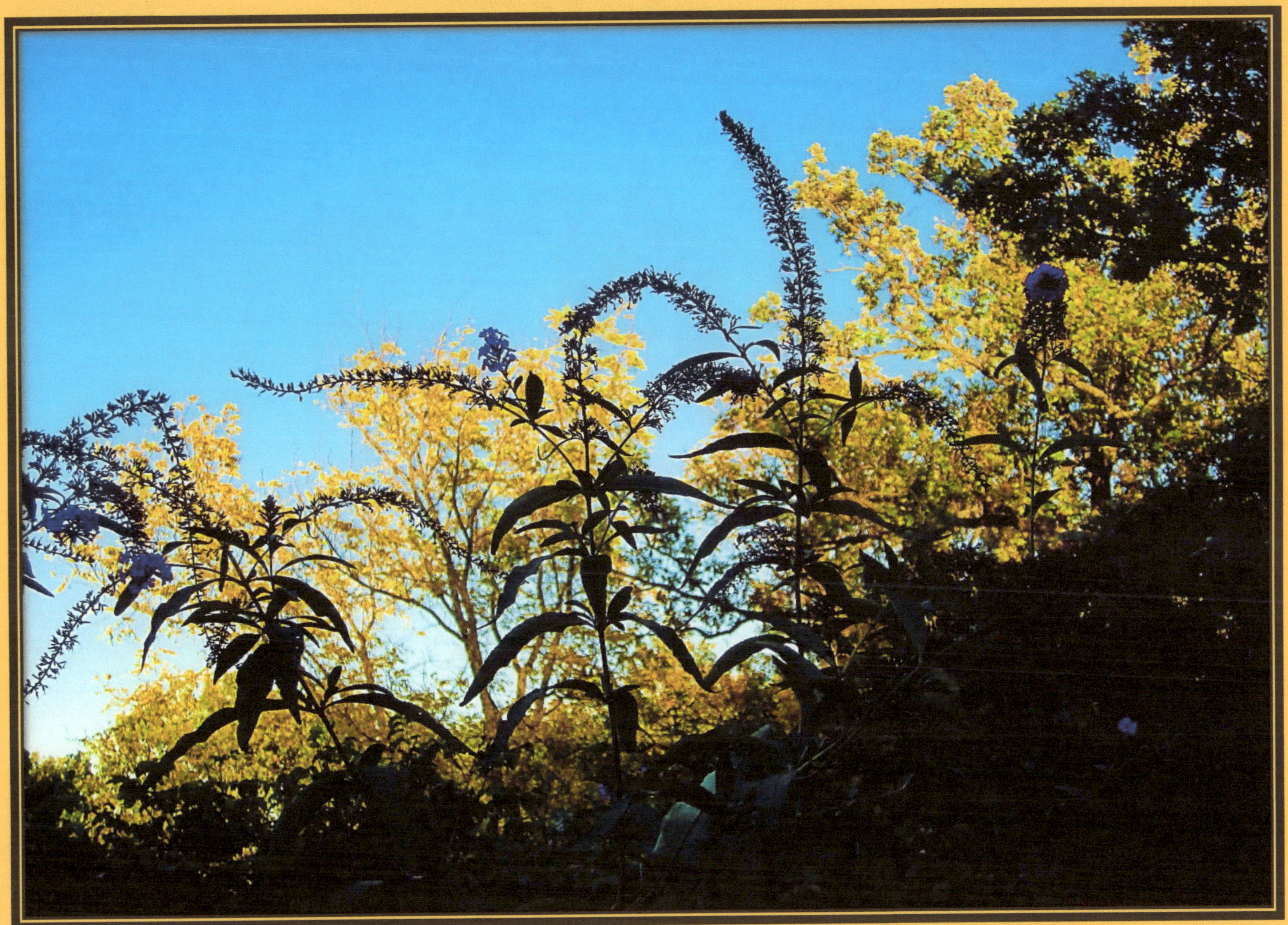

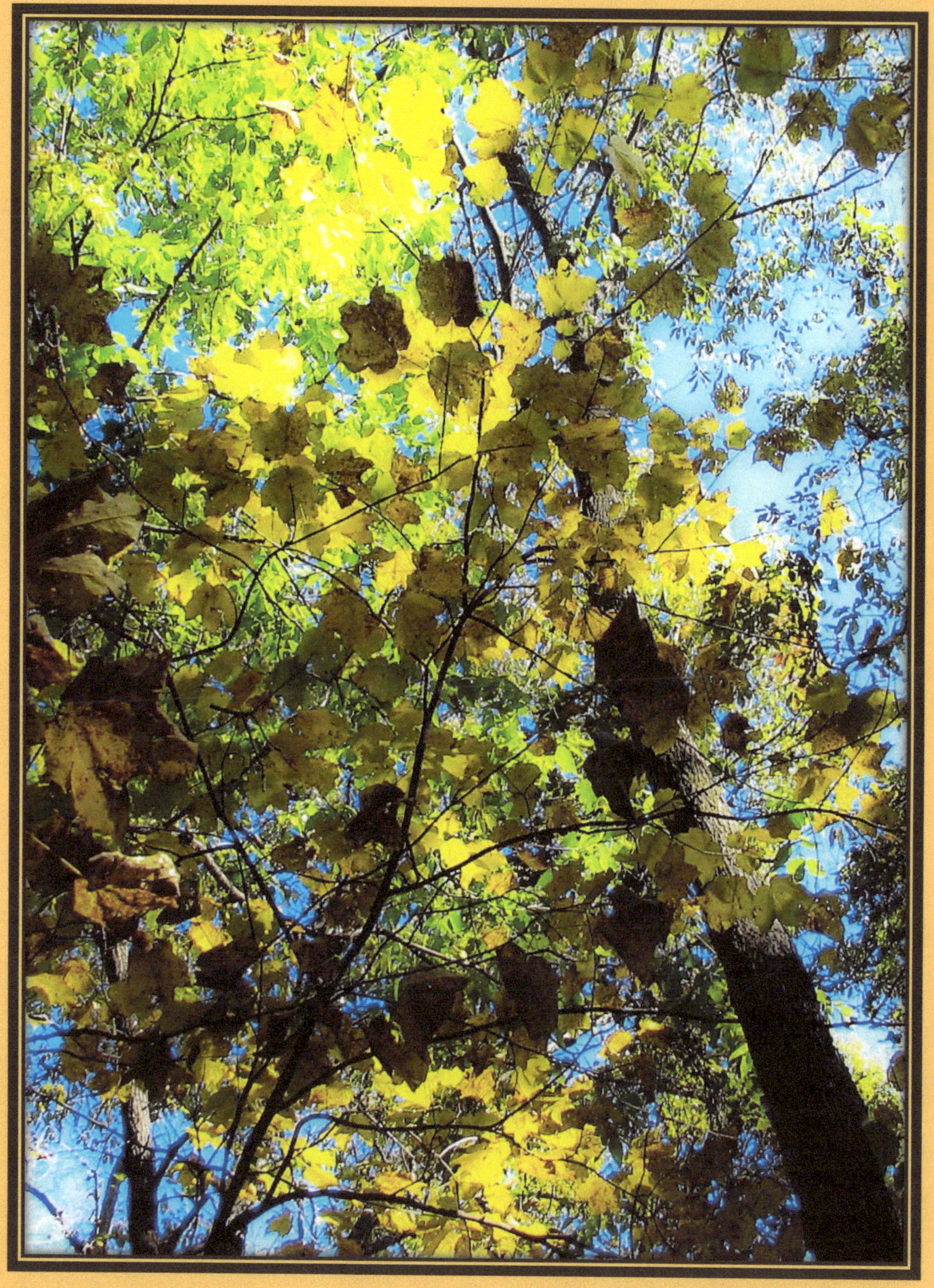

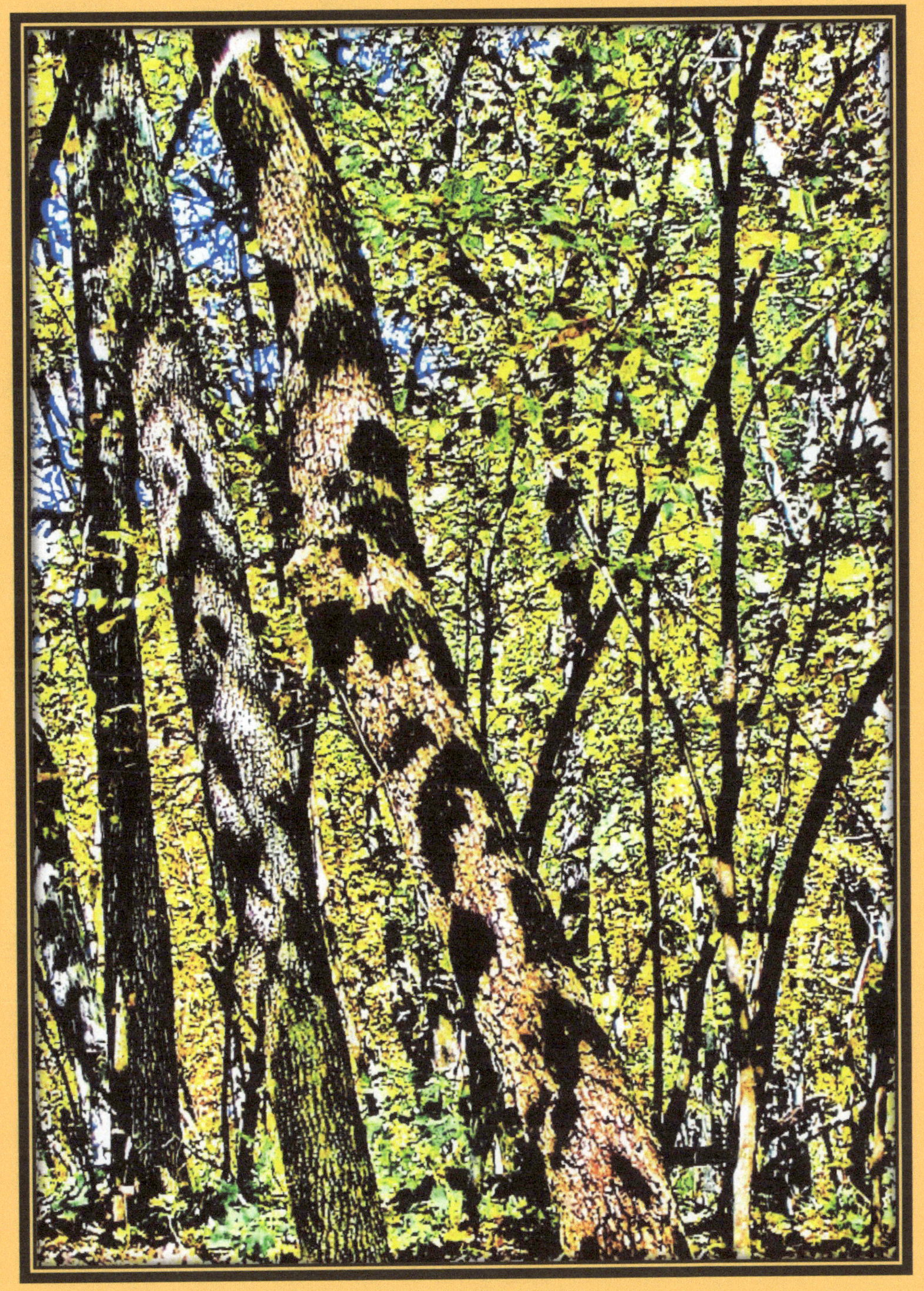

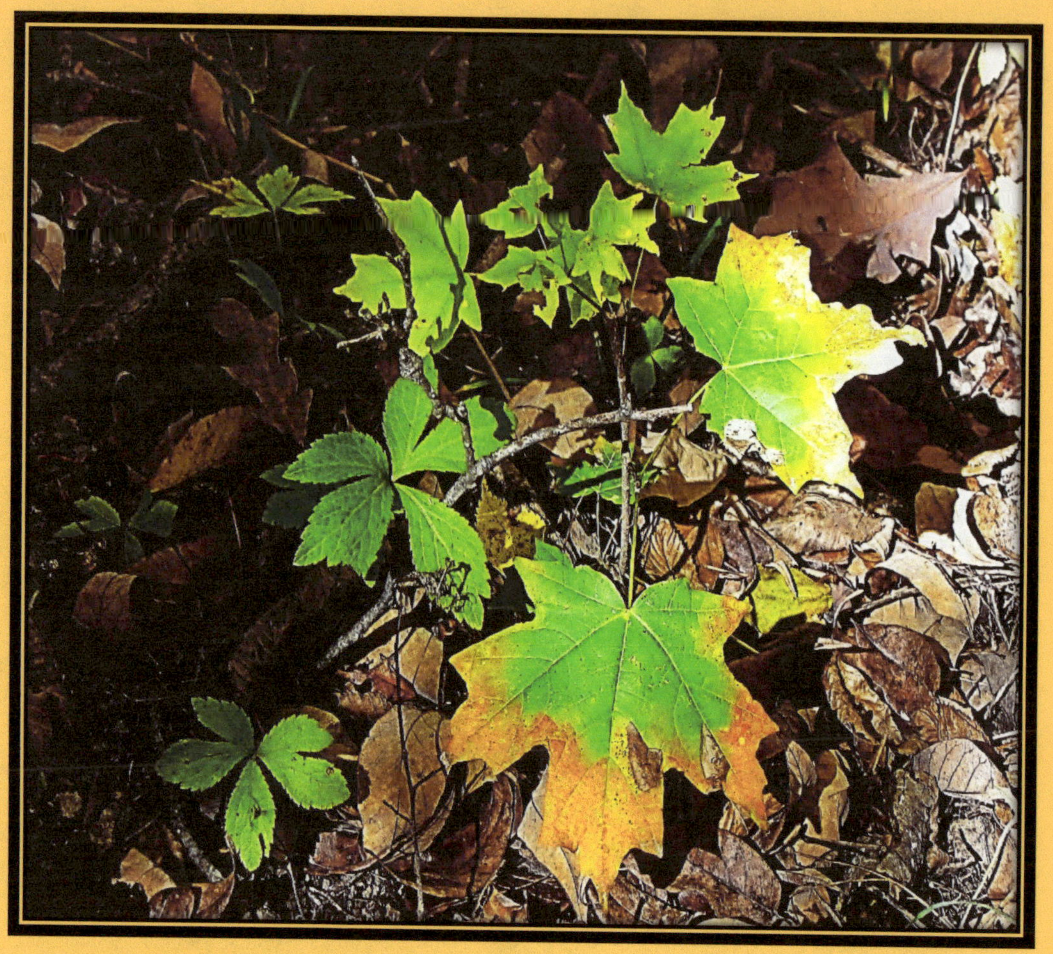

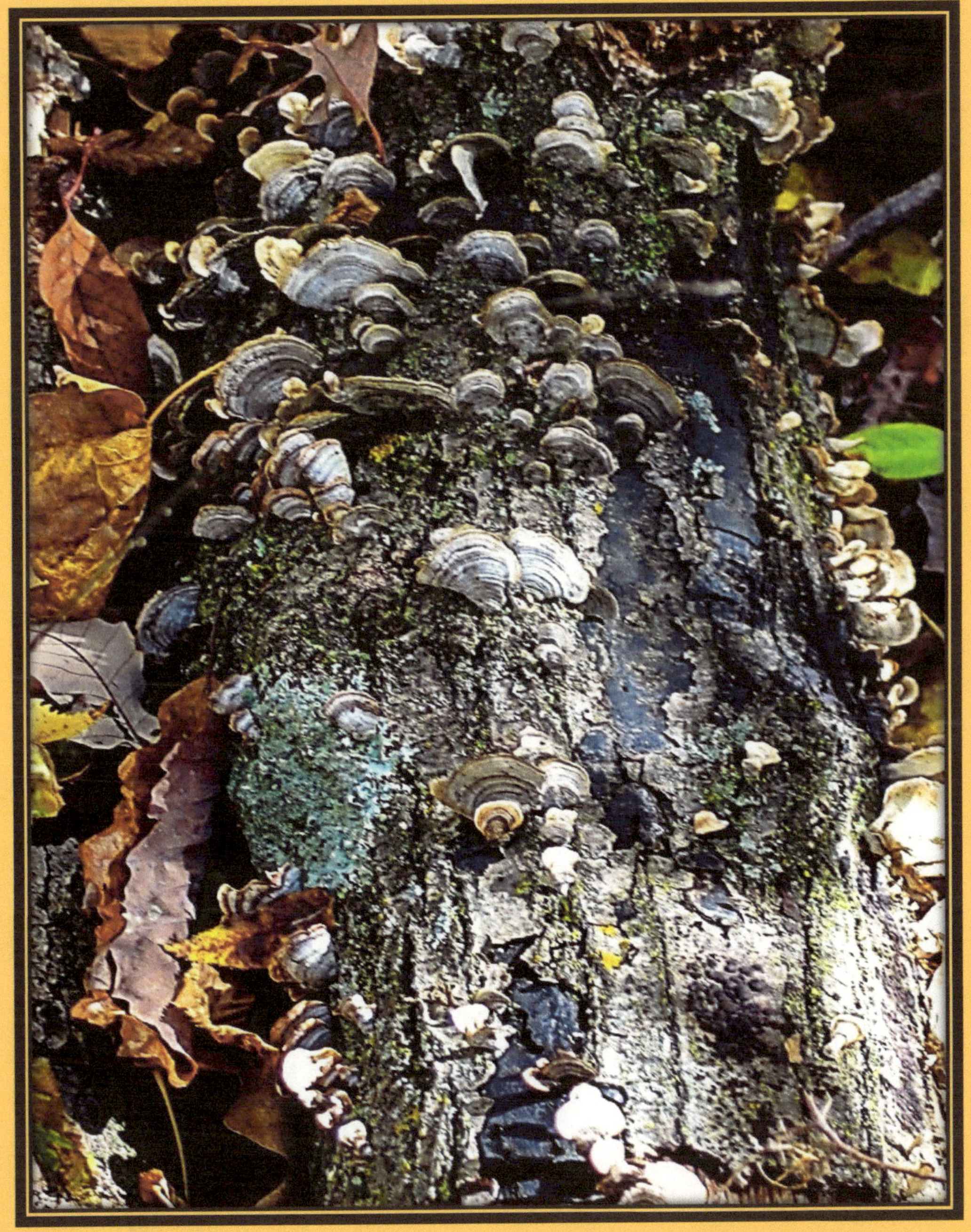

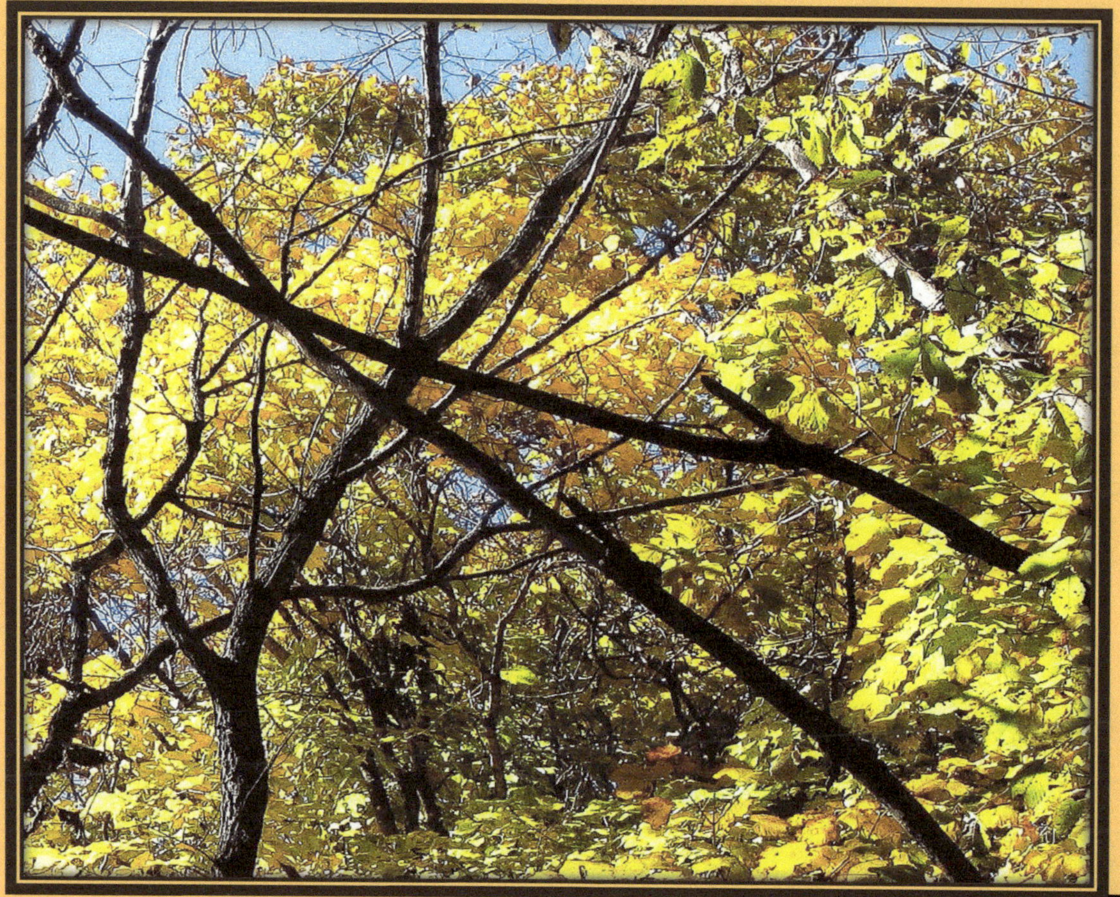

Forest Crossings.

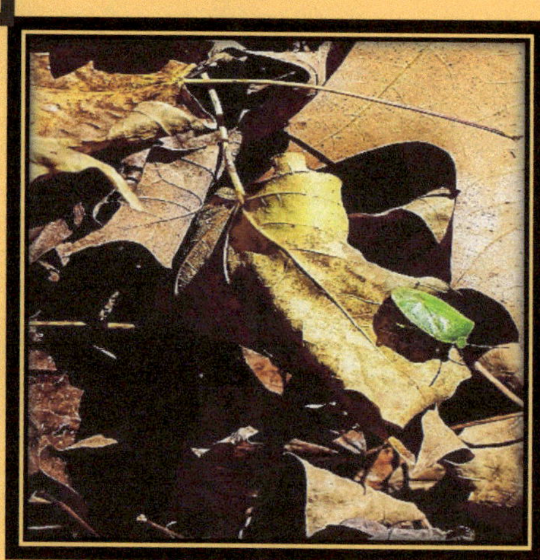

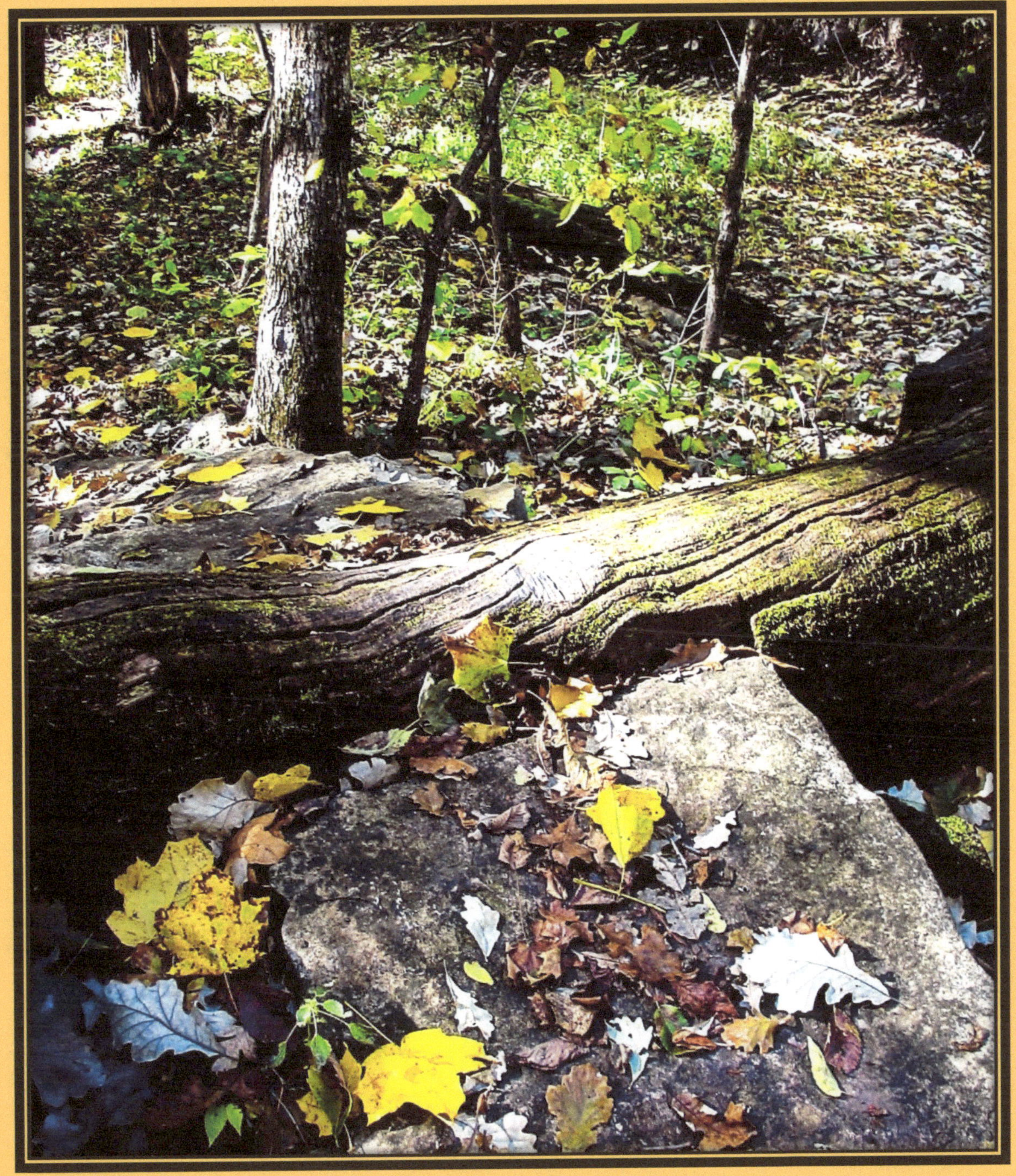

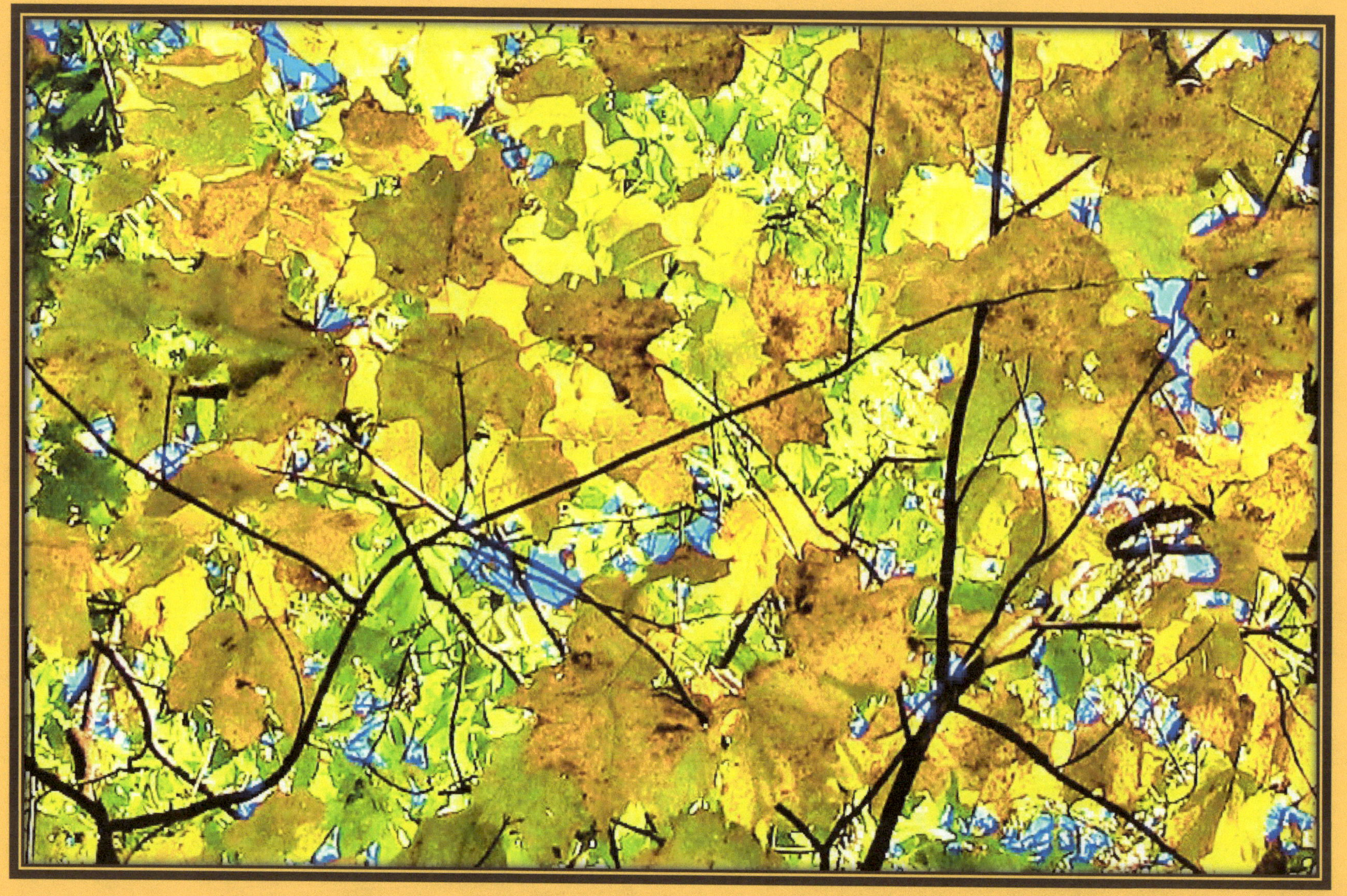

Leafy canopies against the sun glow like stained glass windows.

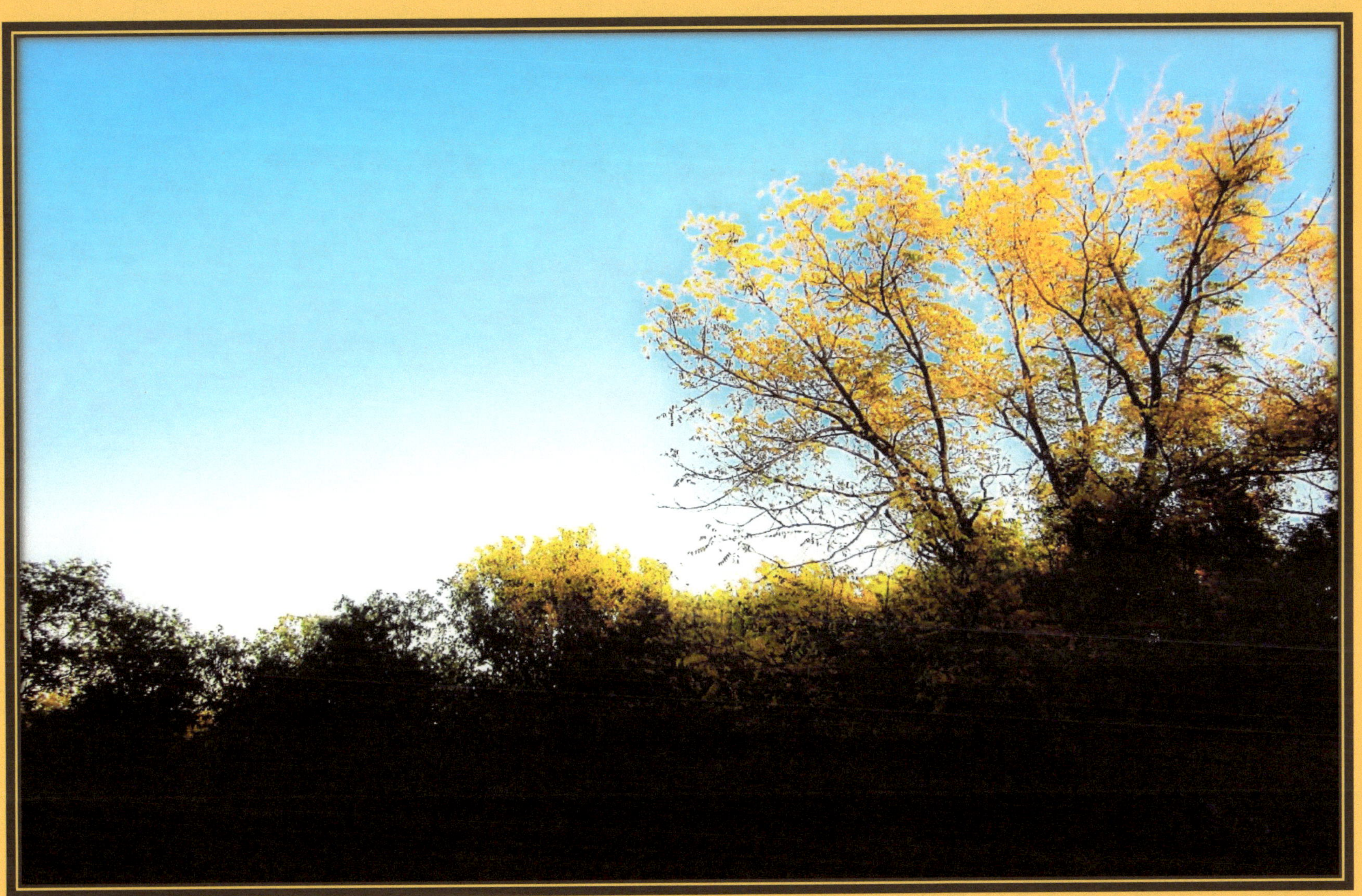

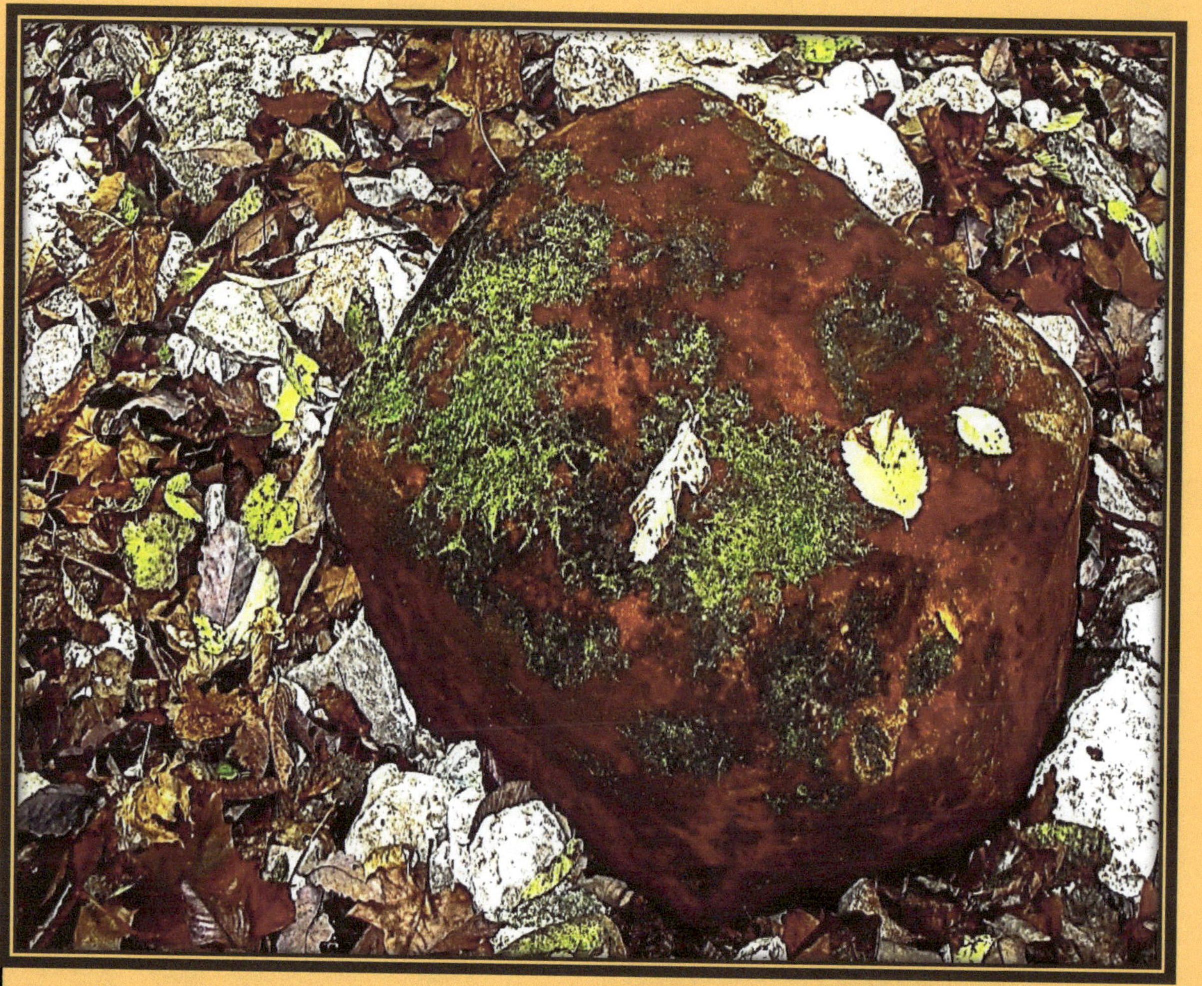

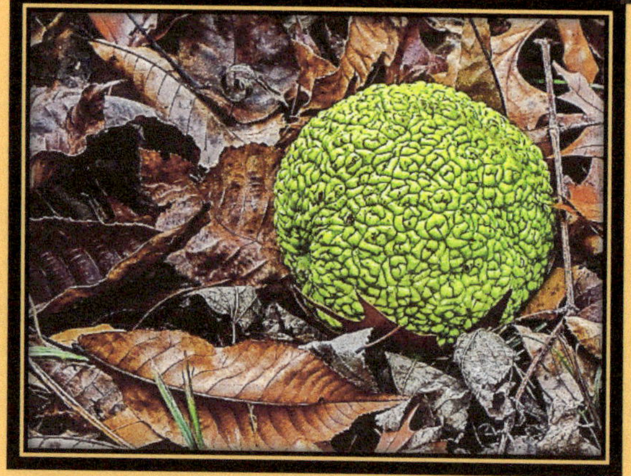

Hedge apple and rock with clingers.

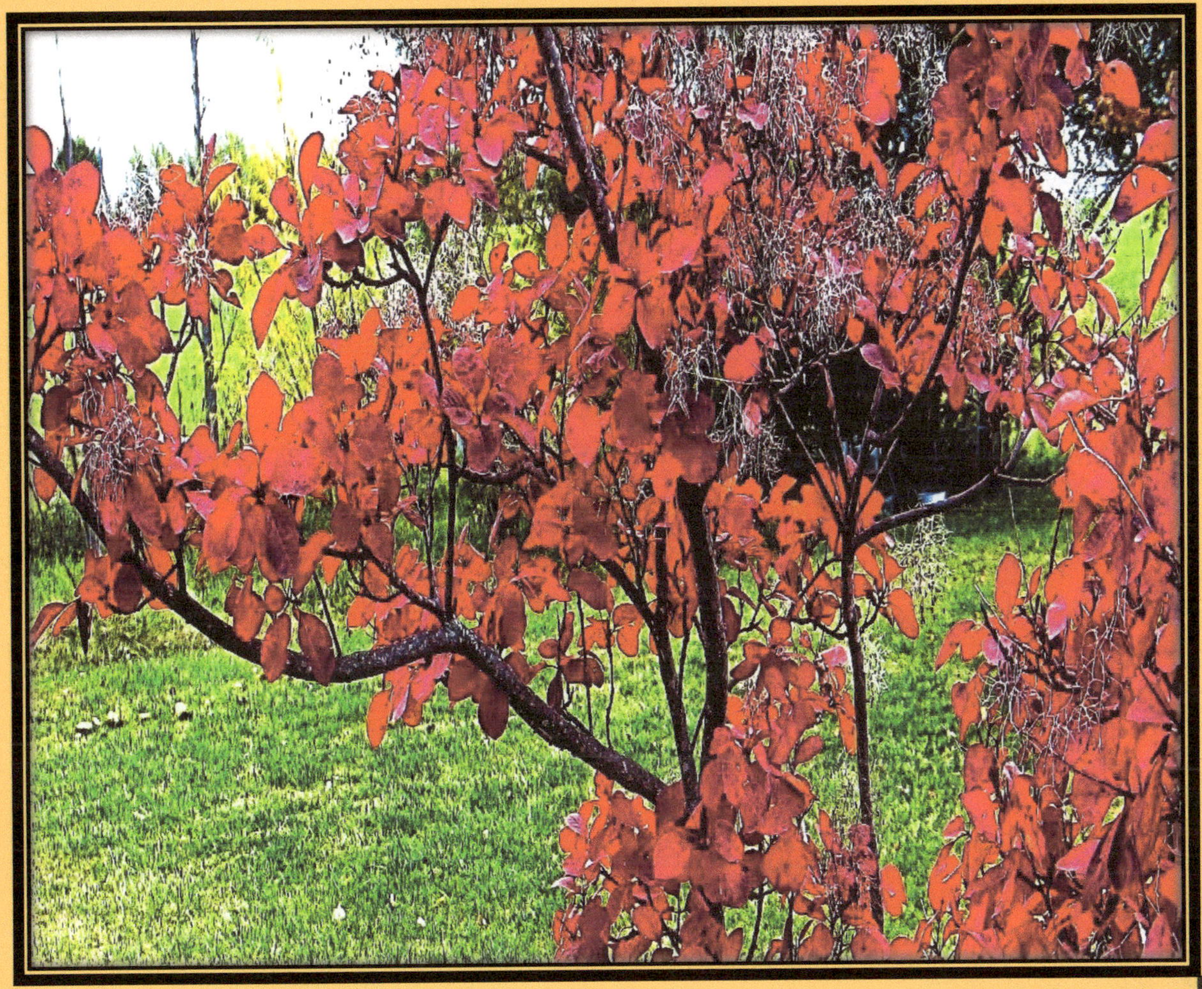

Pastoral excellence.

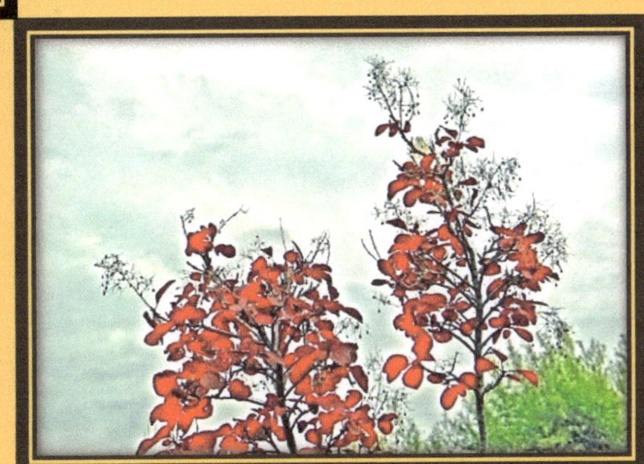

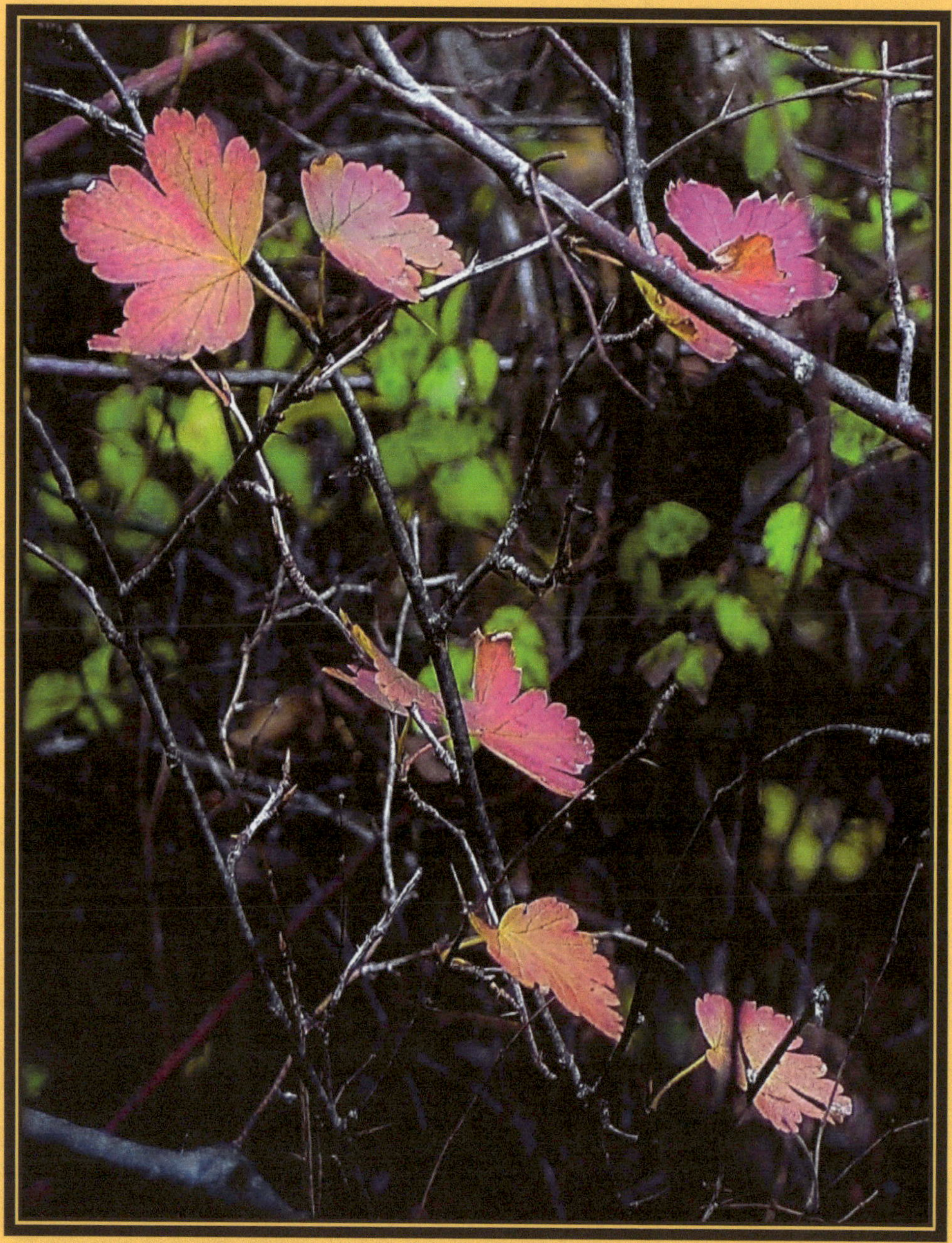

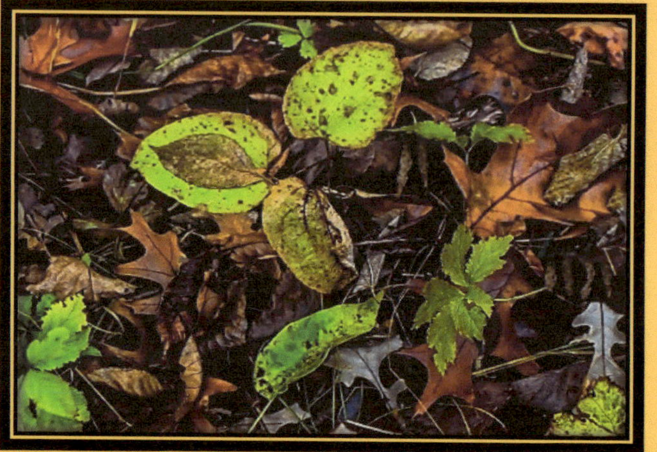

Forest
floors
seem
soft
below.

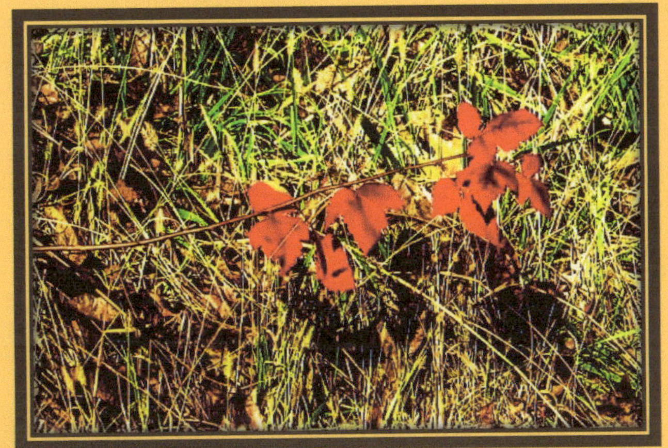

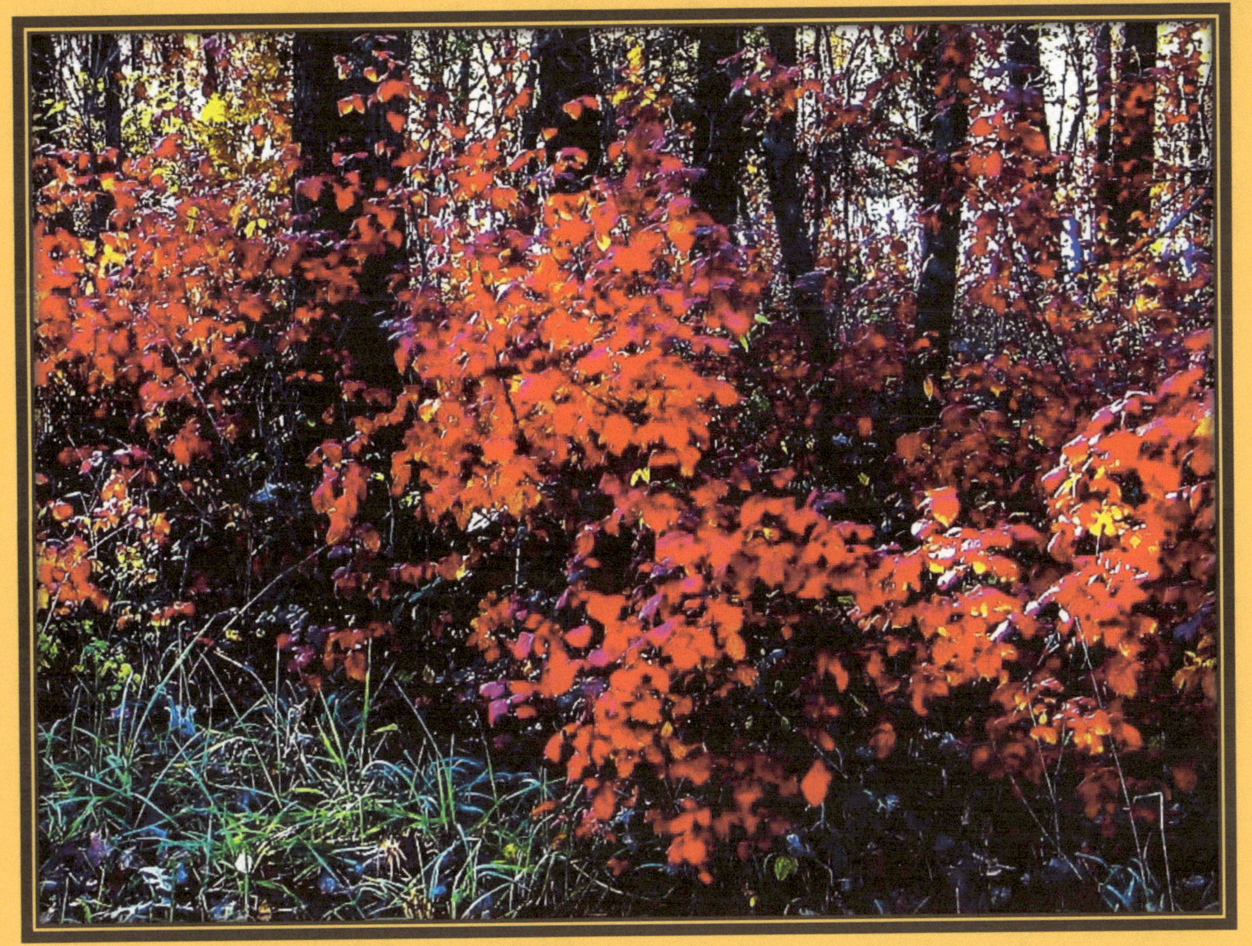

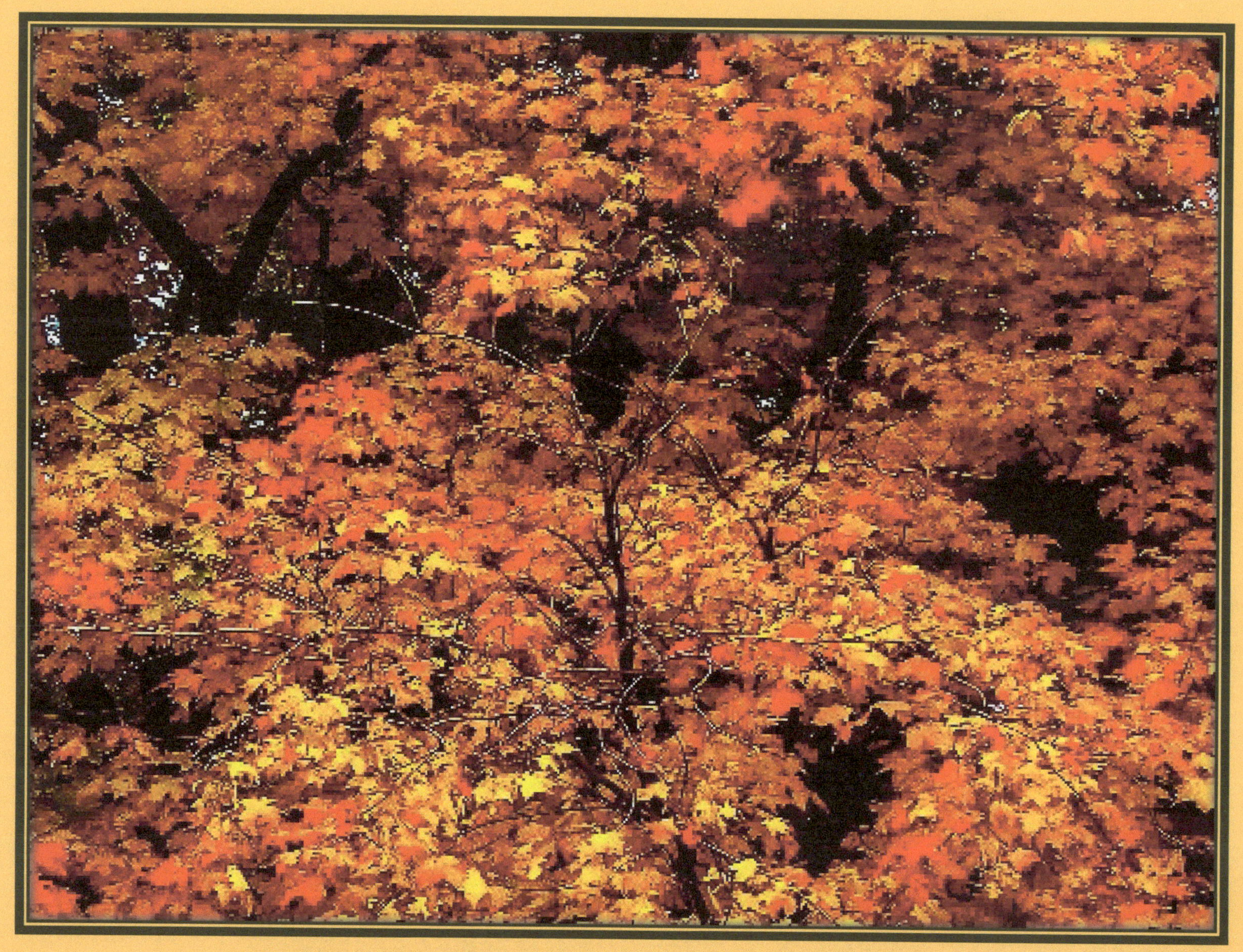

Above, treetops display flamboyant finery.

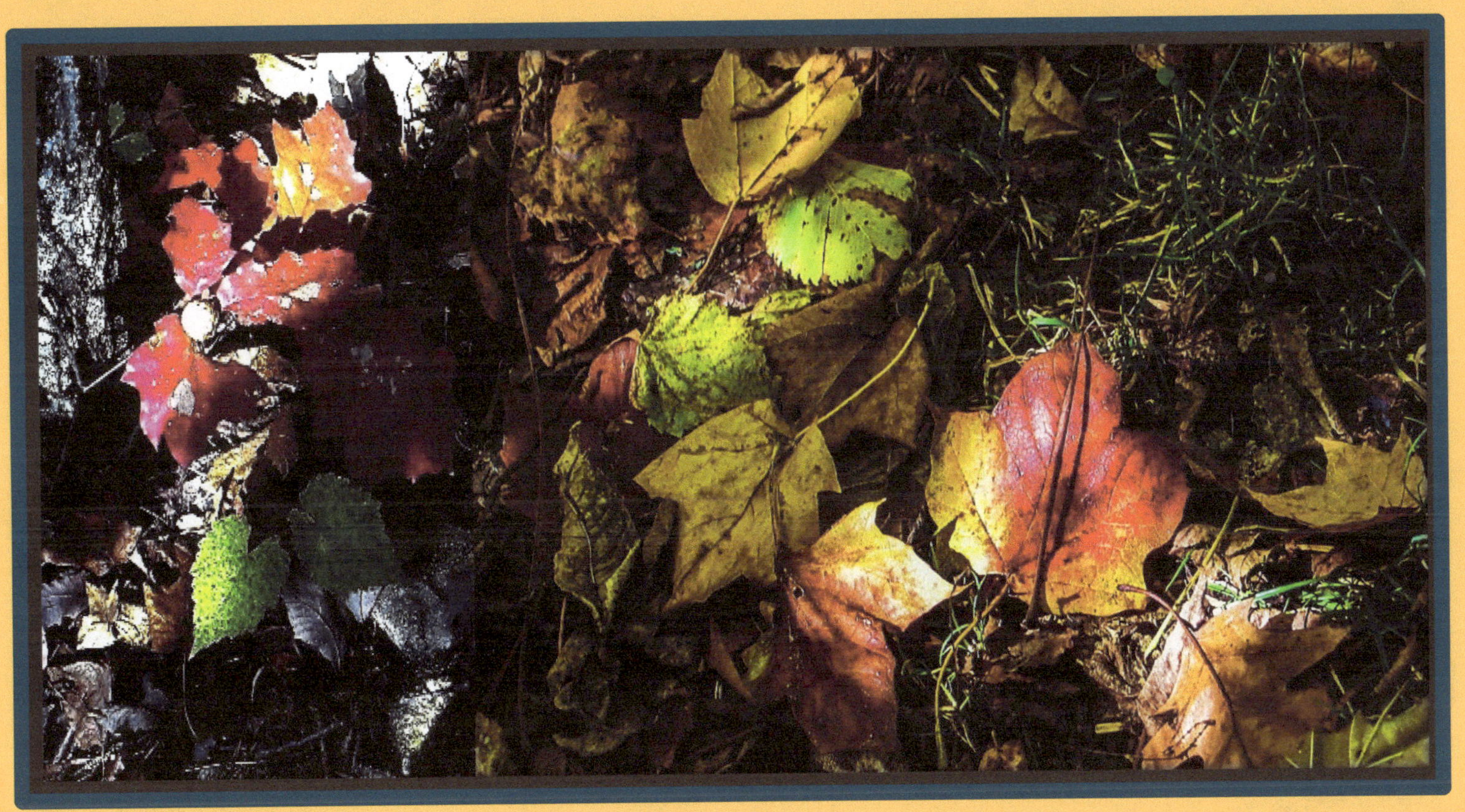

Millions of leaves peak in riotous colors.

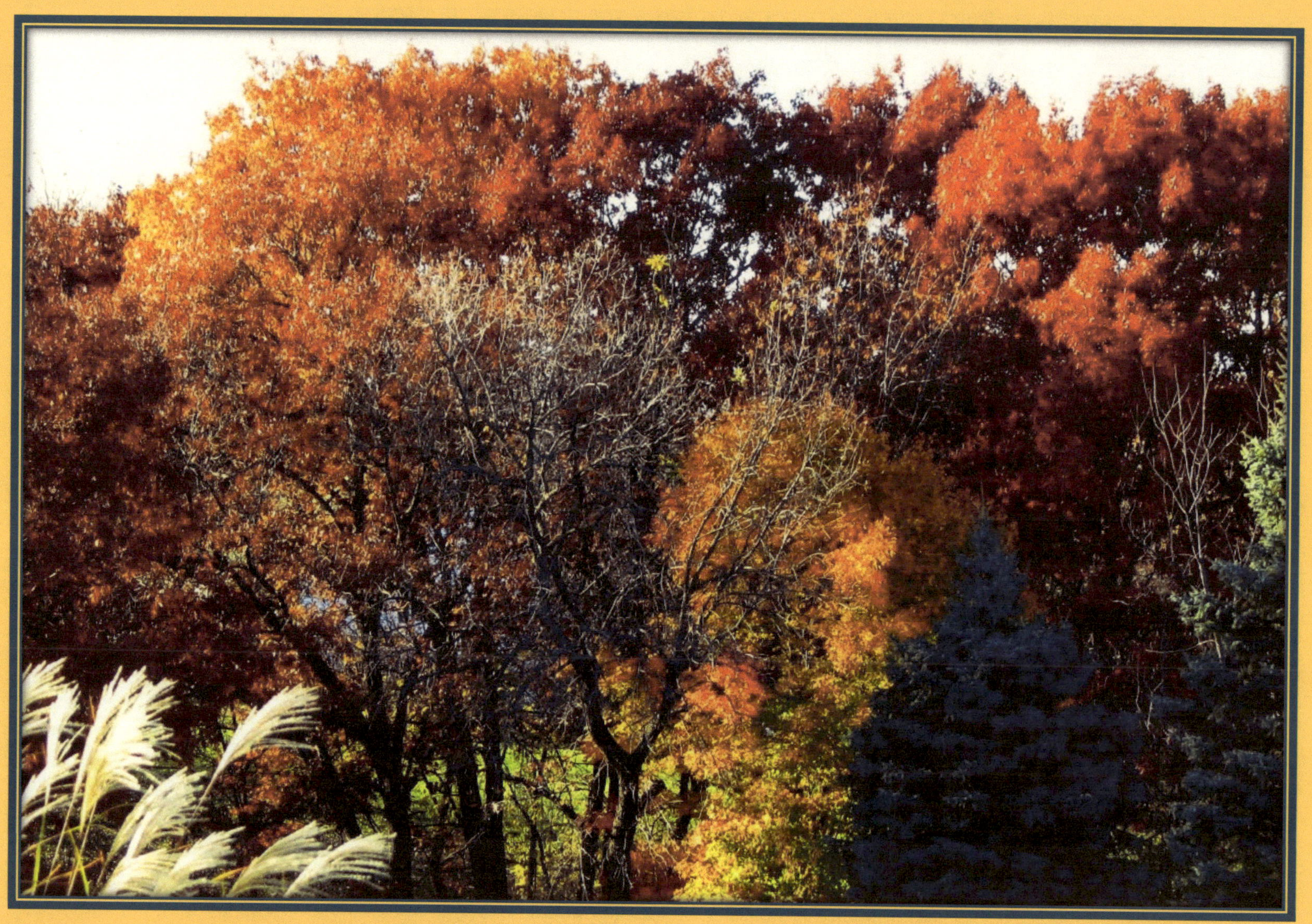

Then, they fall.

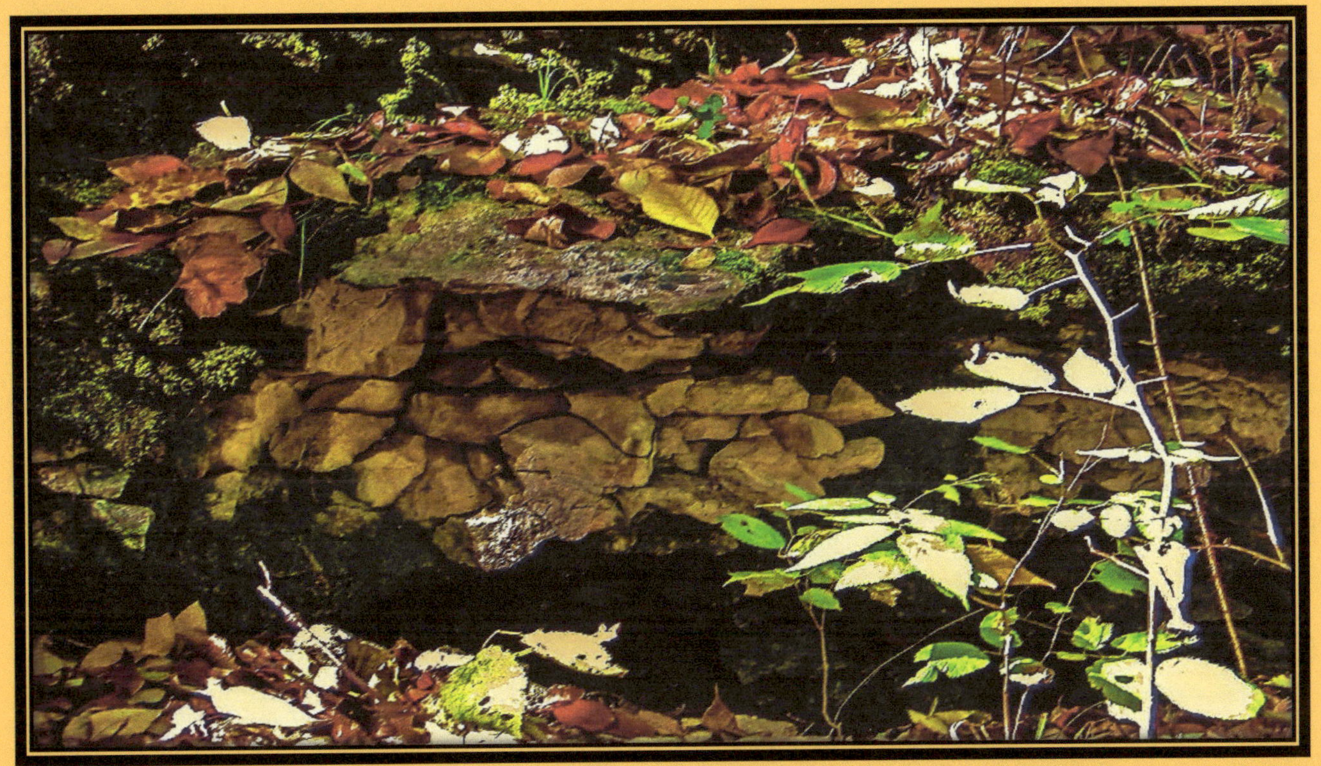

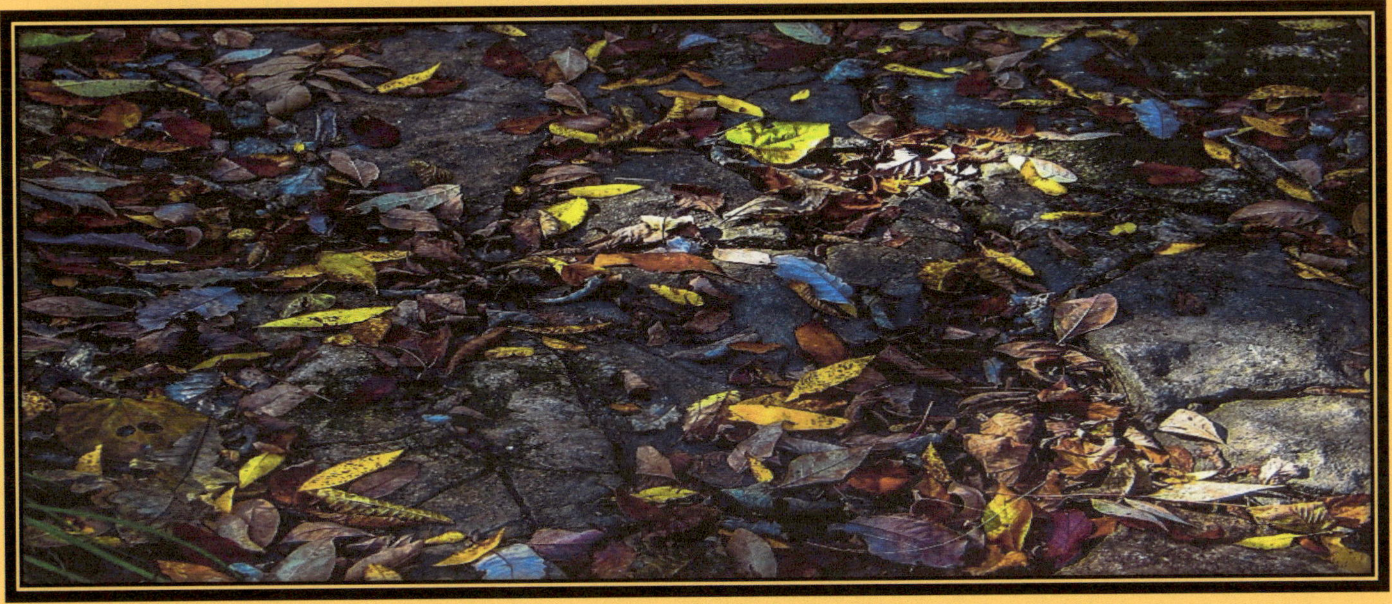

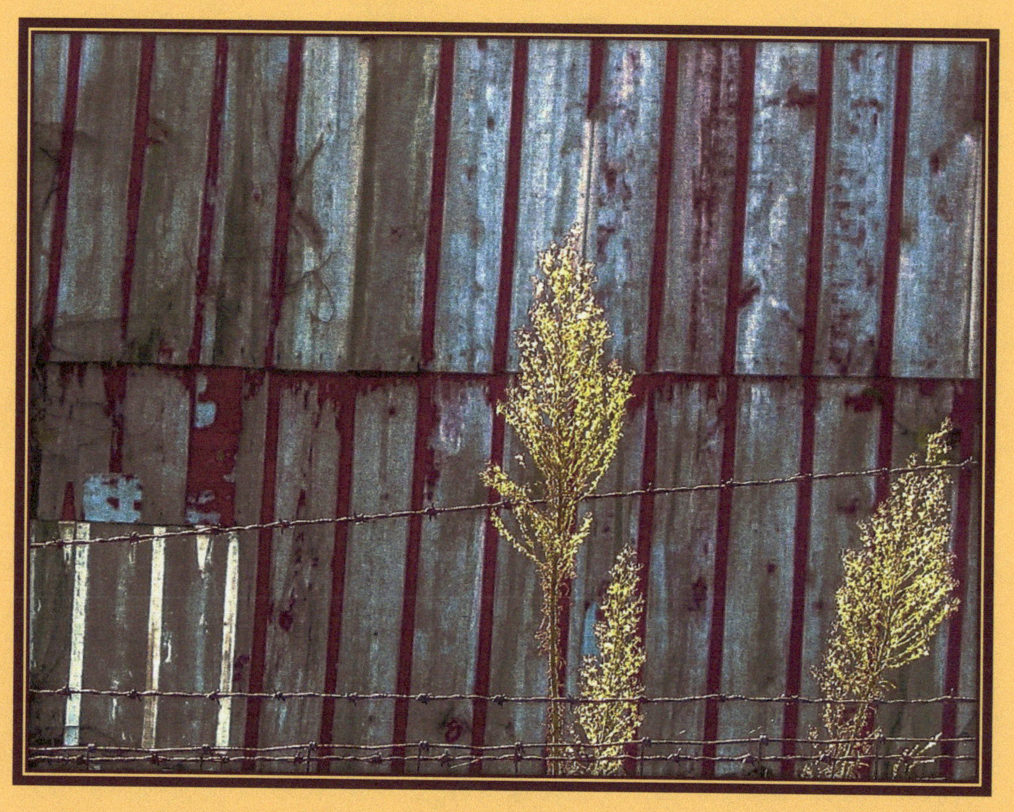

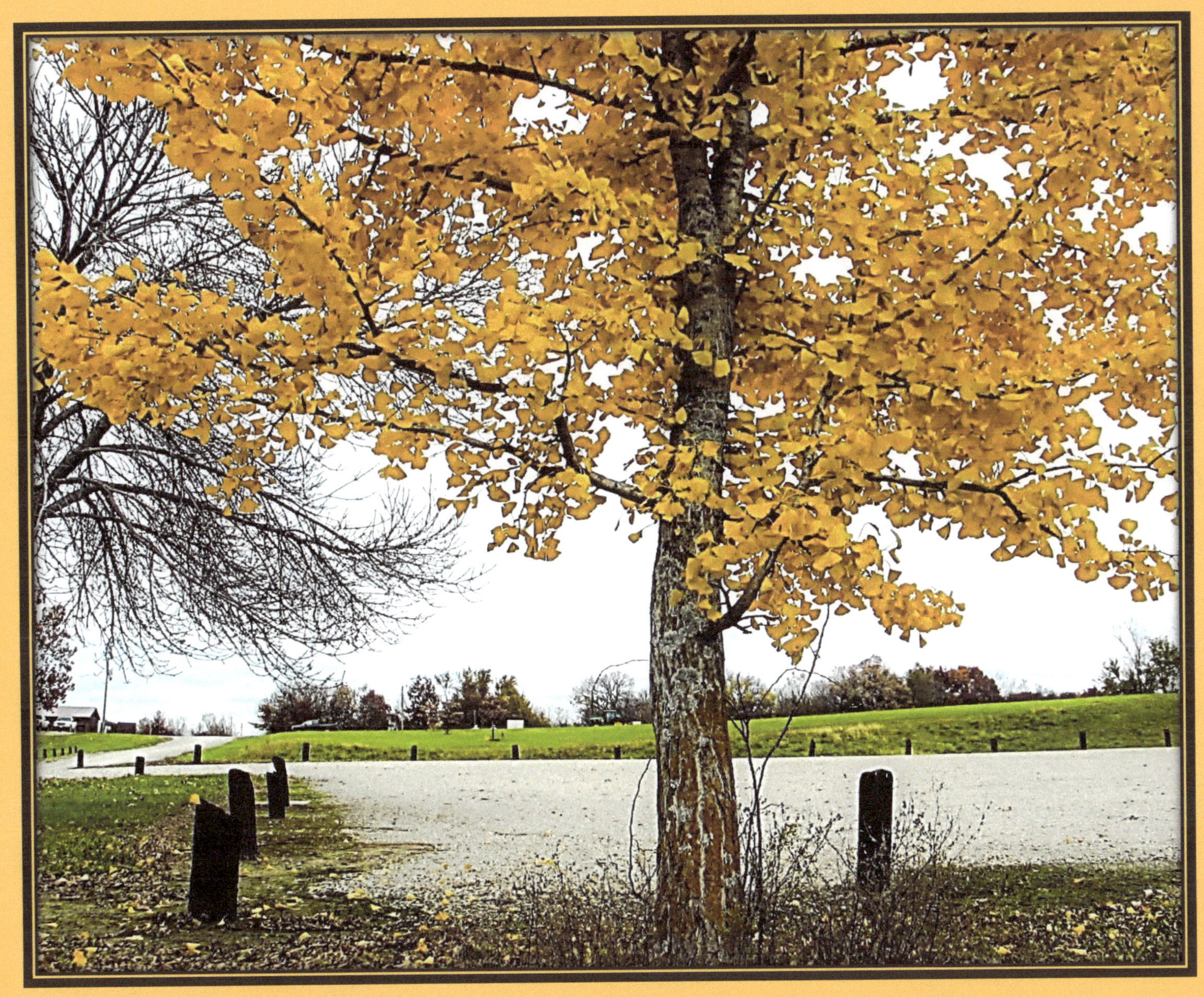

The long-lived, golden-fanned Ginko tree prevails.

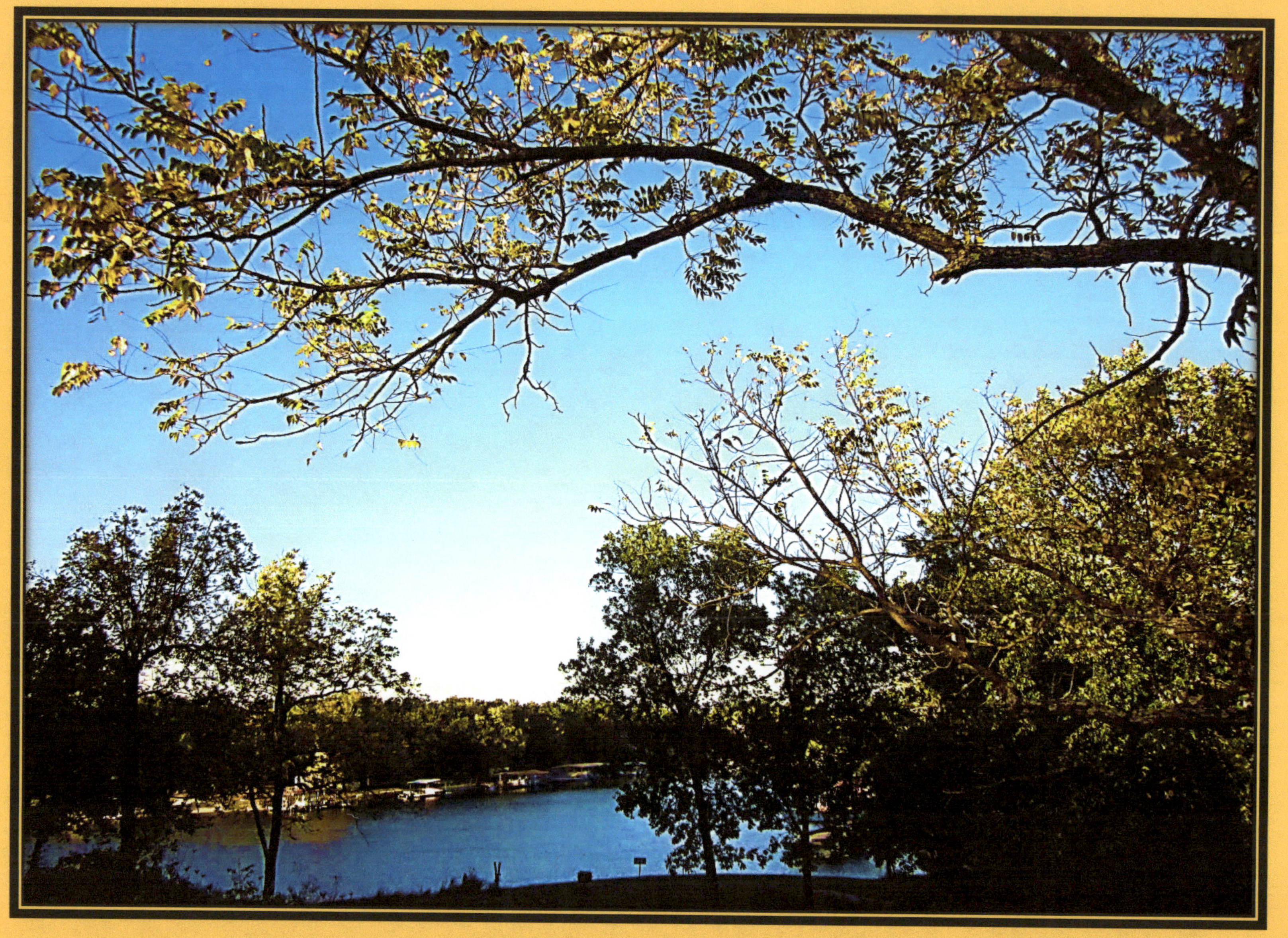

Songbirds and other living things gather at the lake.

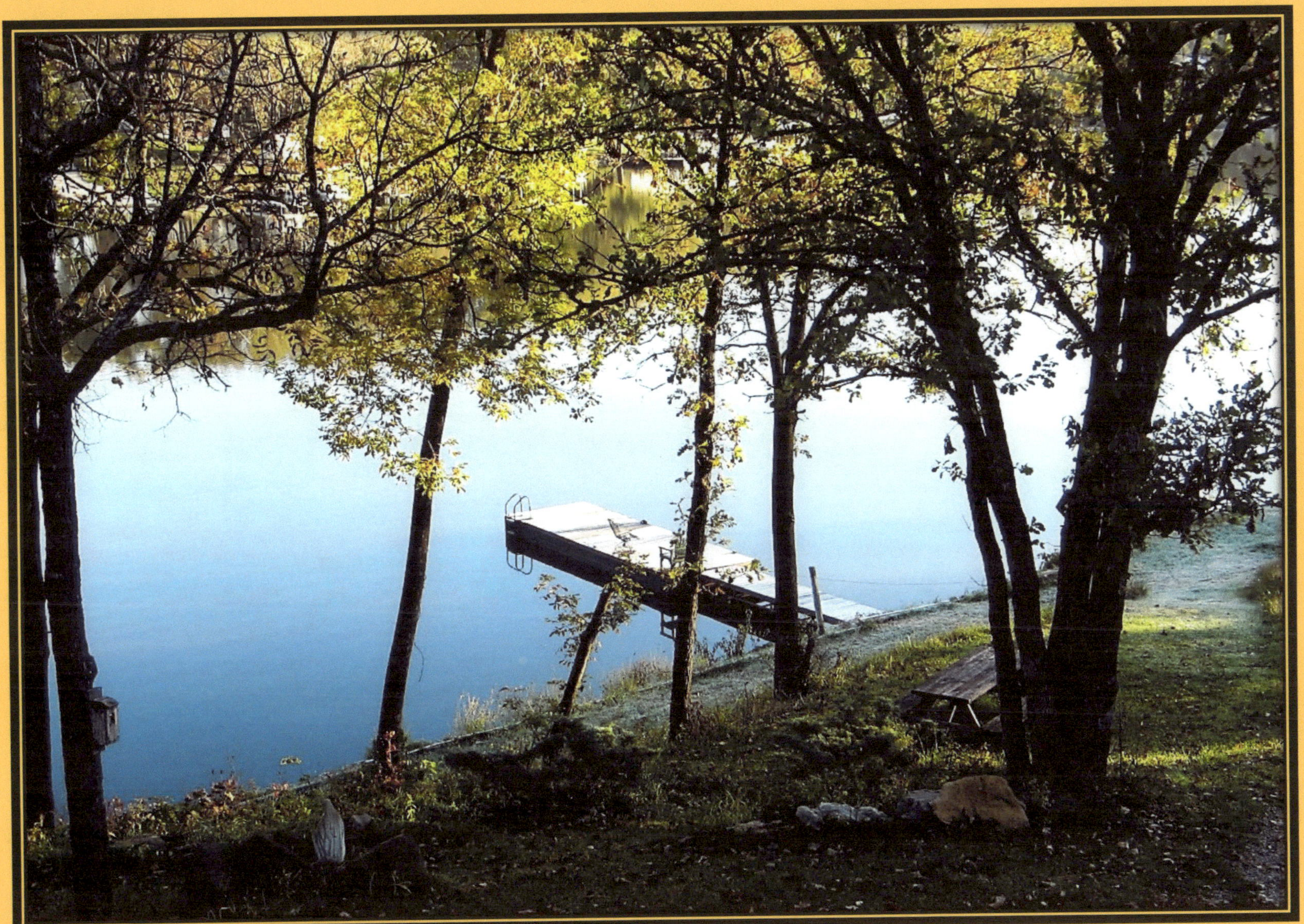

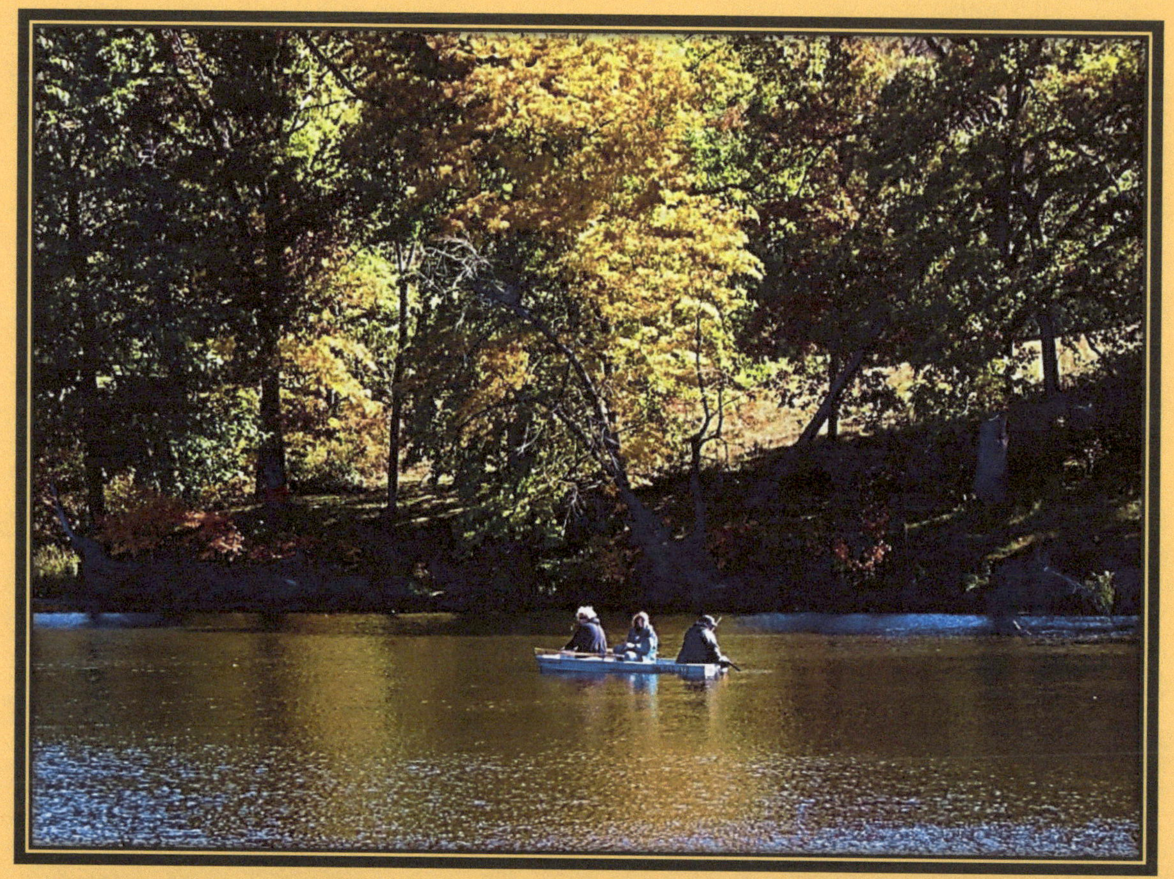

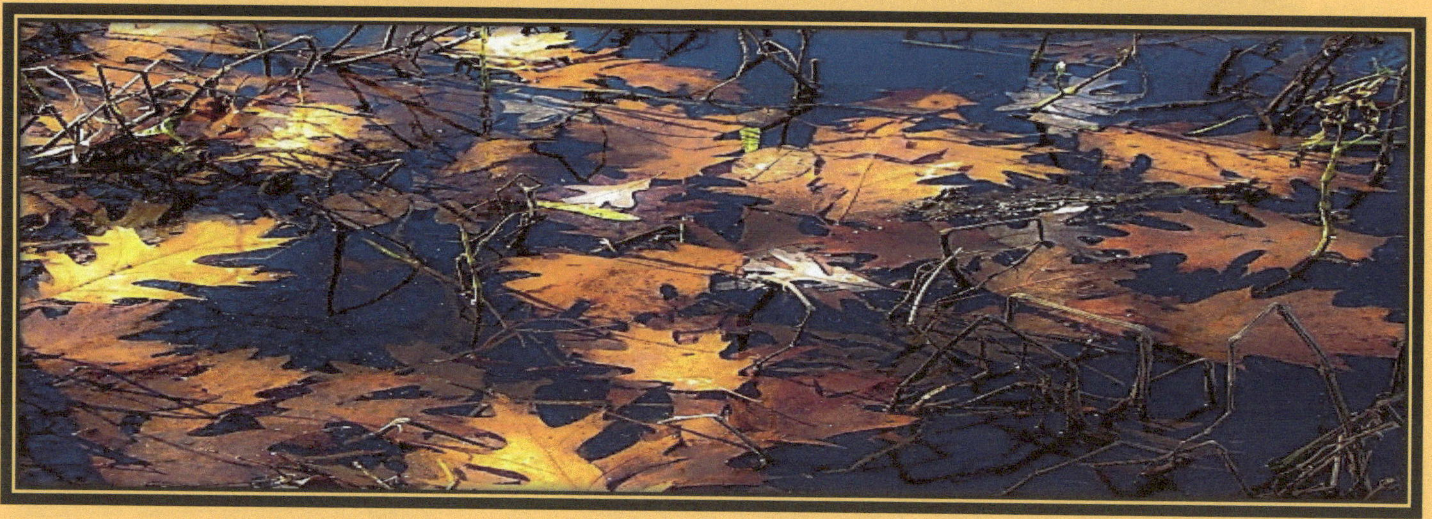

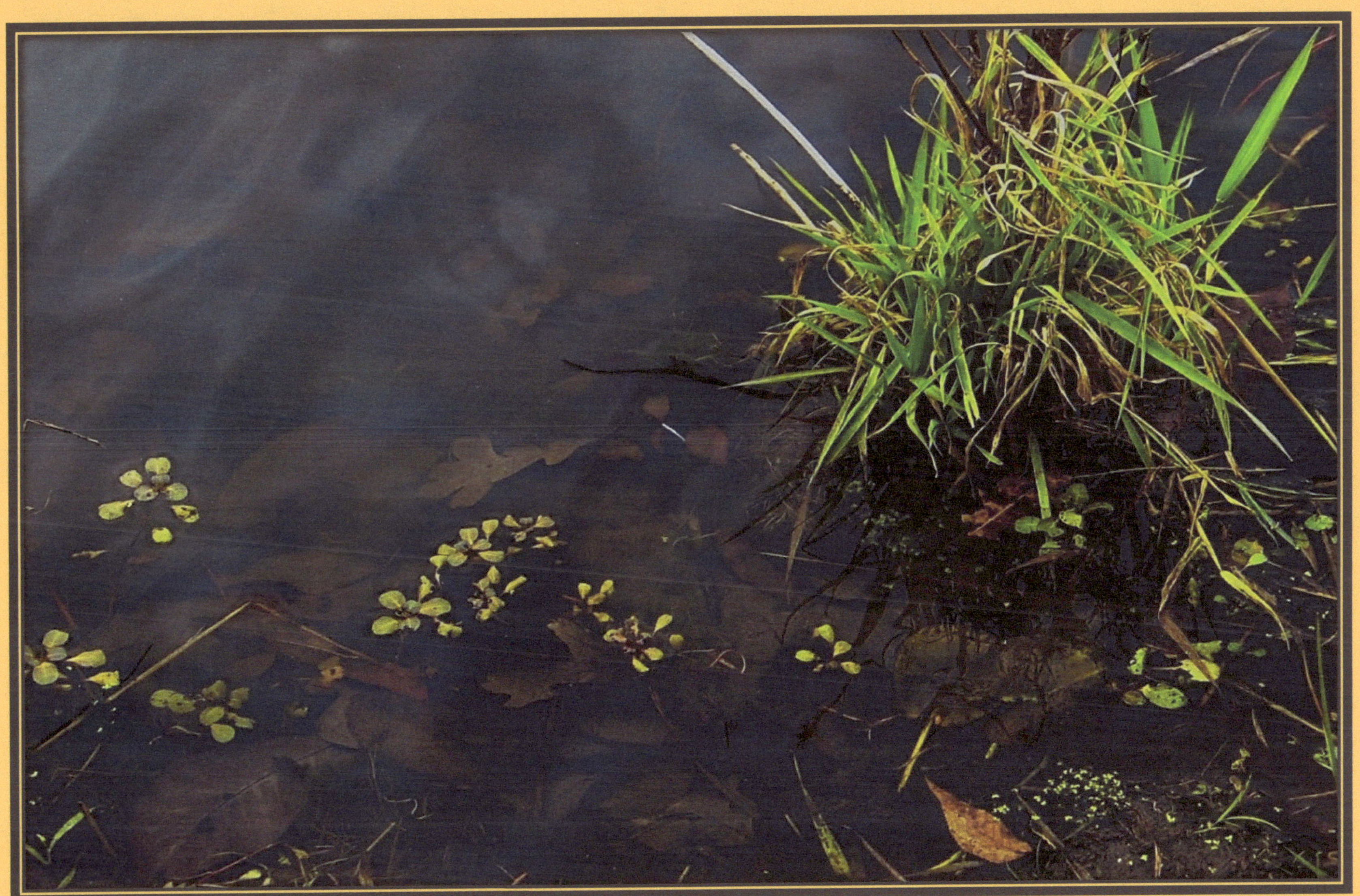

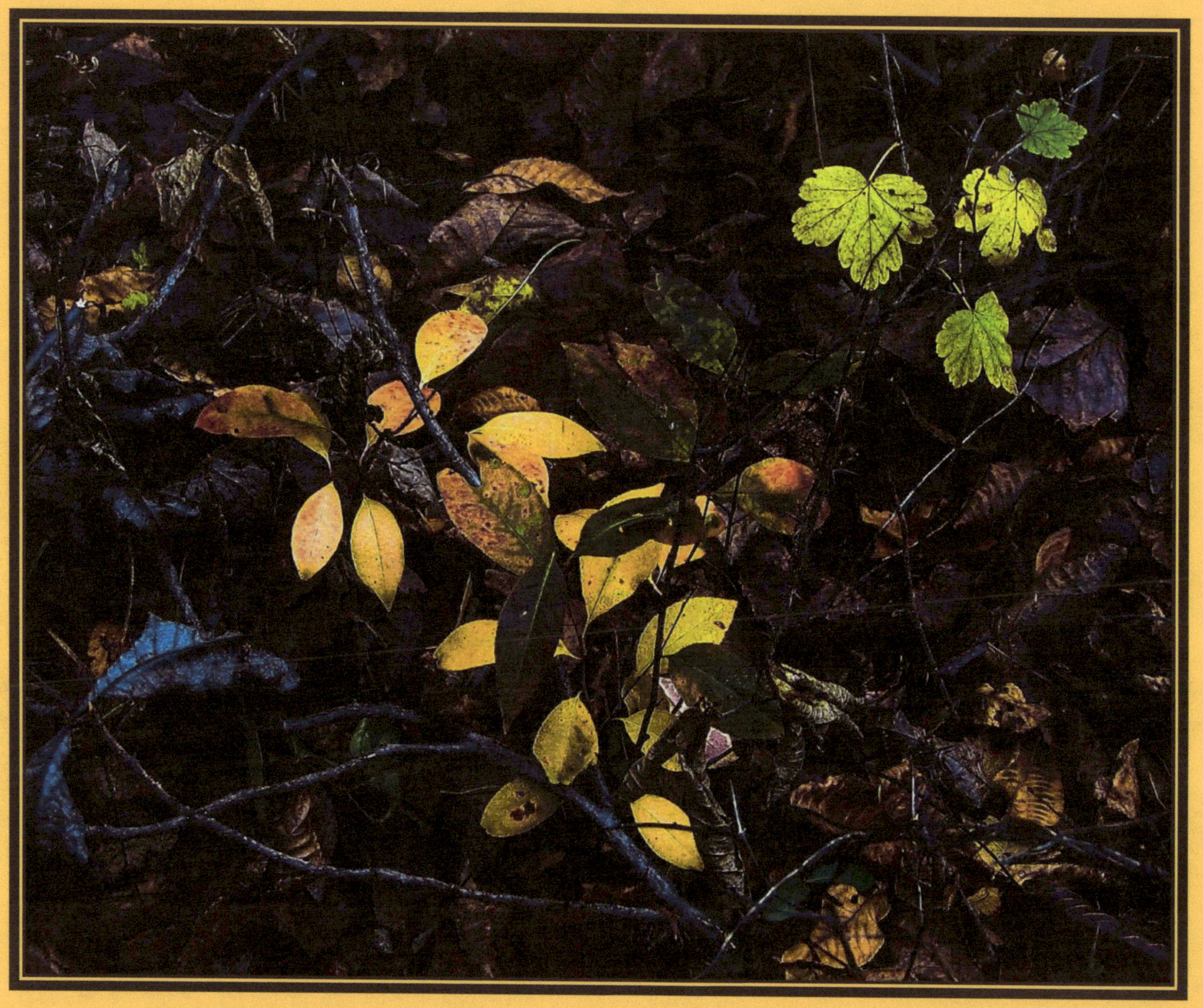

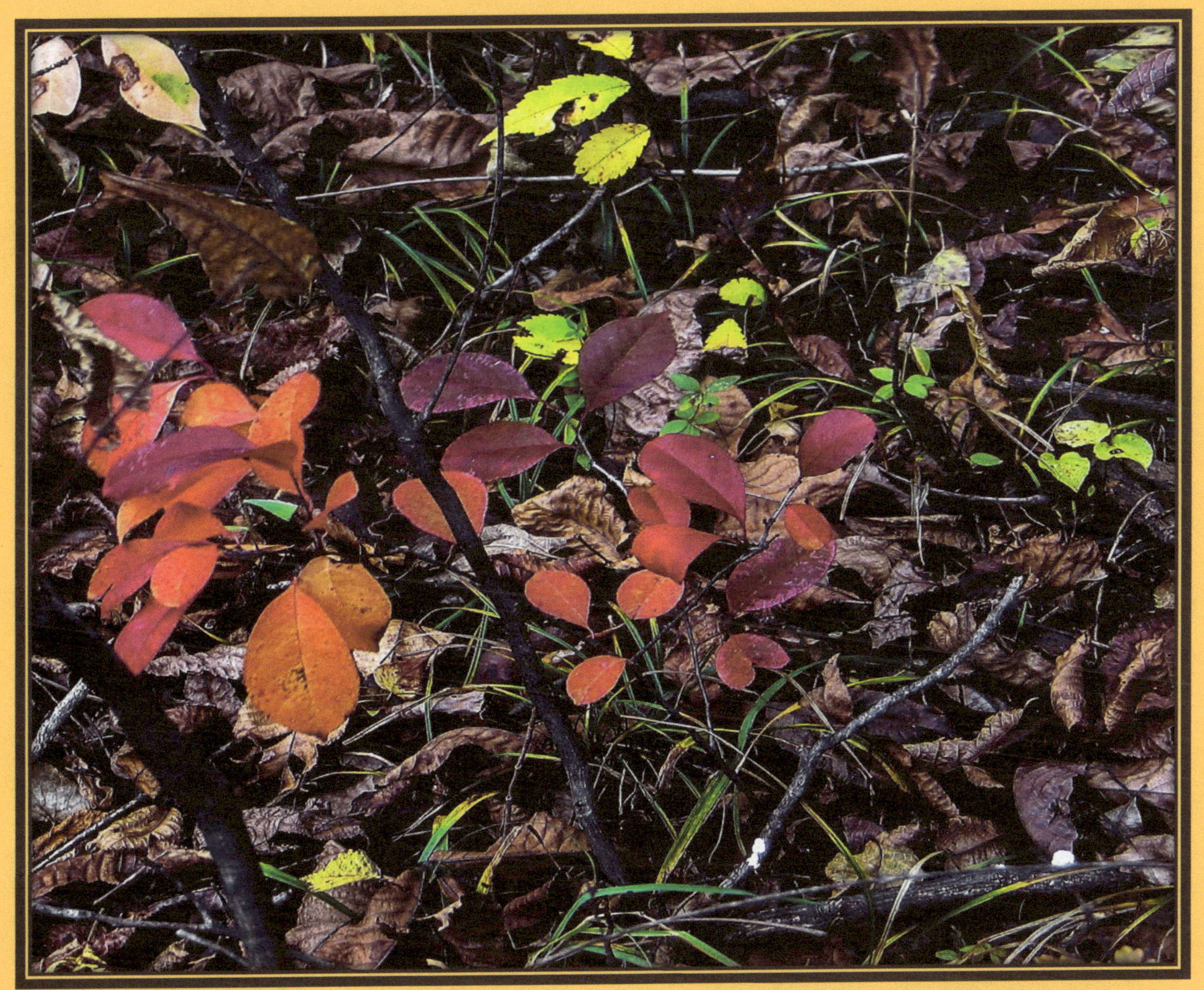

Demure beneath.

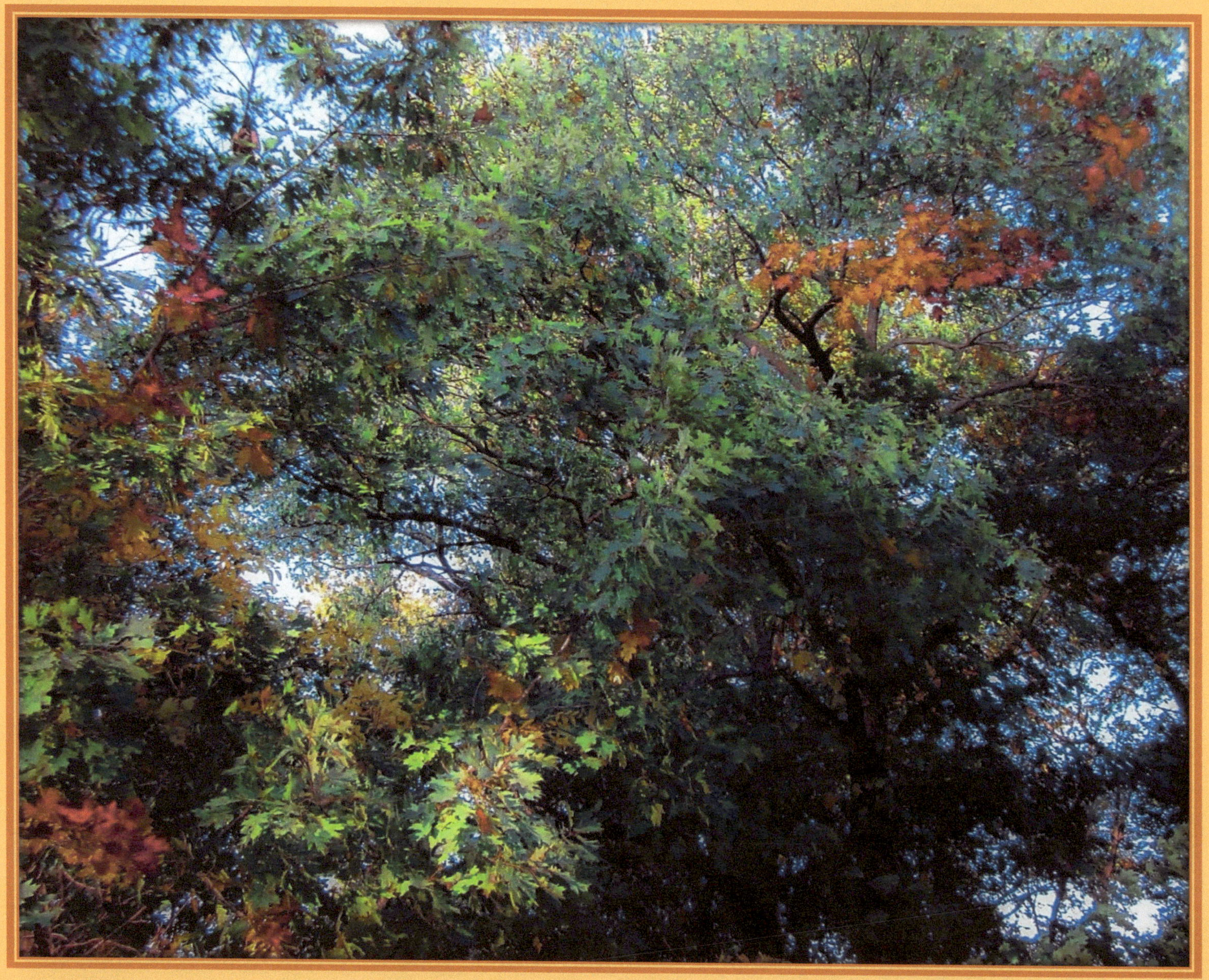

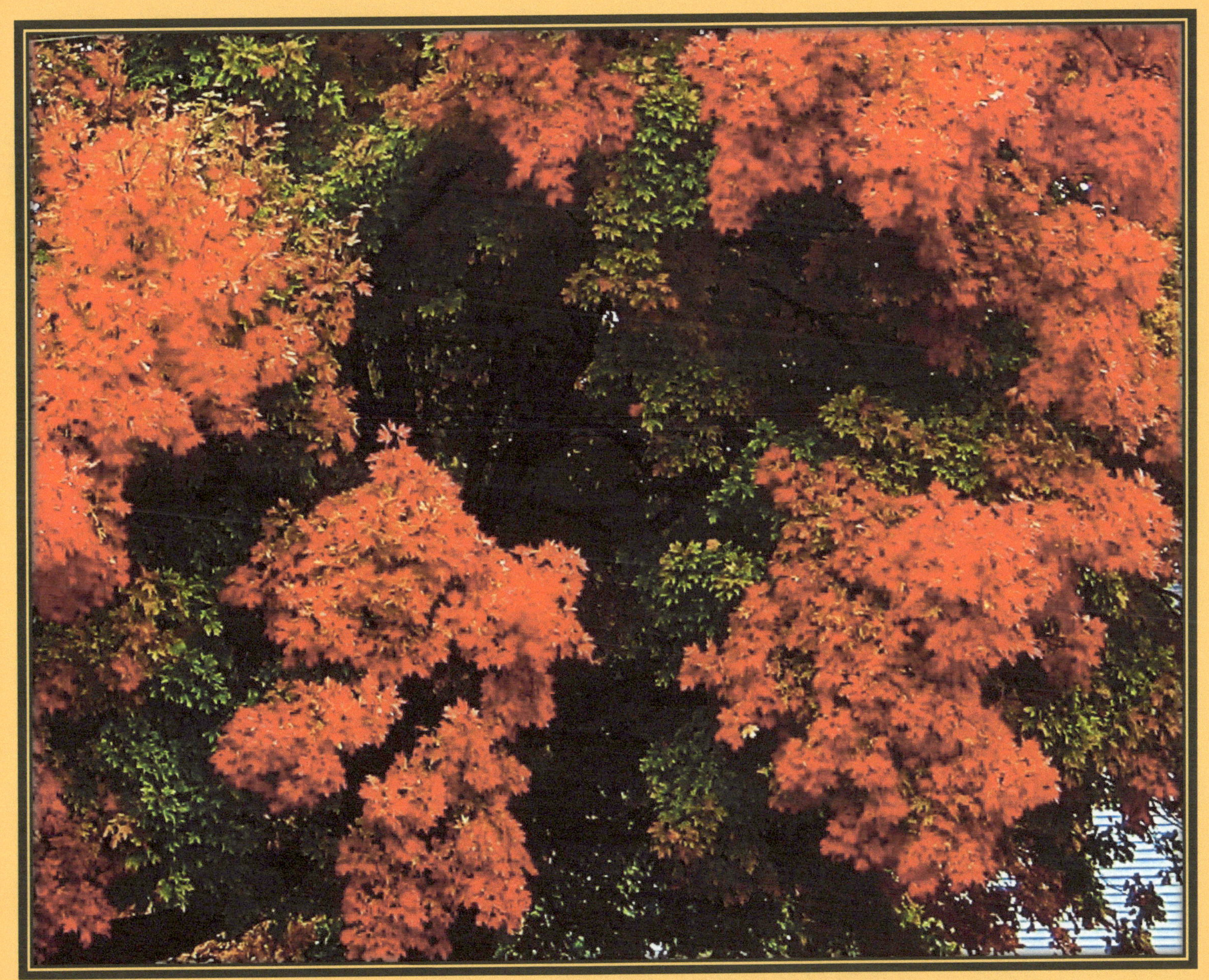

Striking above.

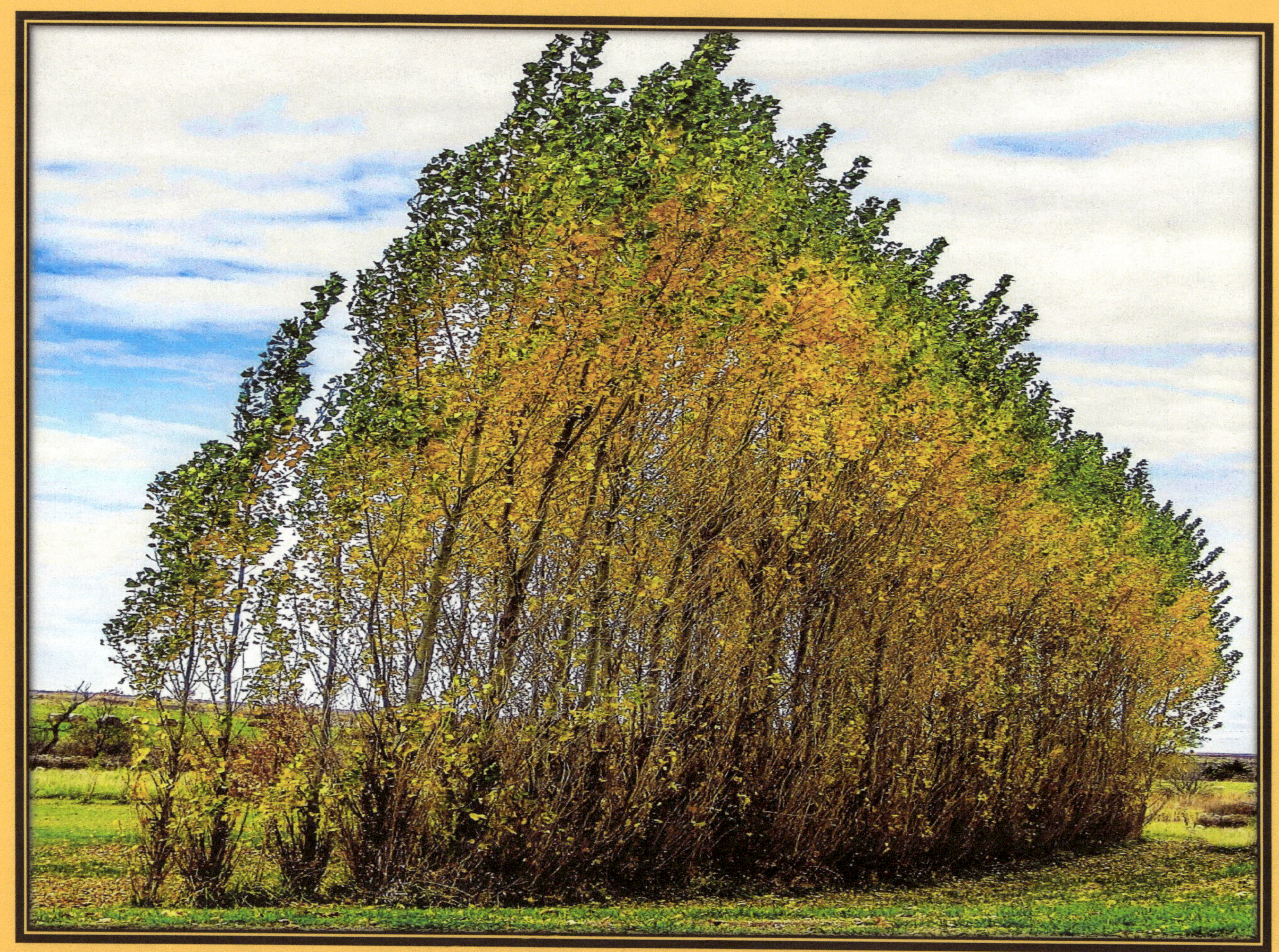

Dynamic.

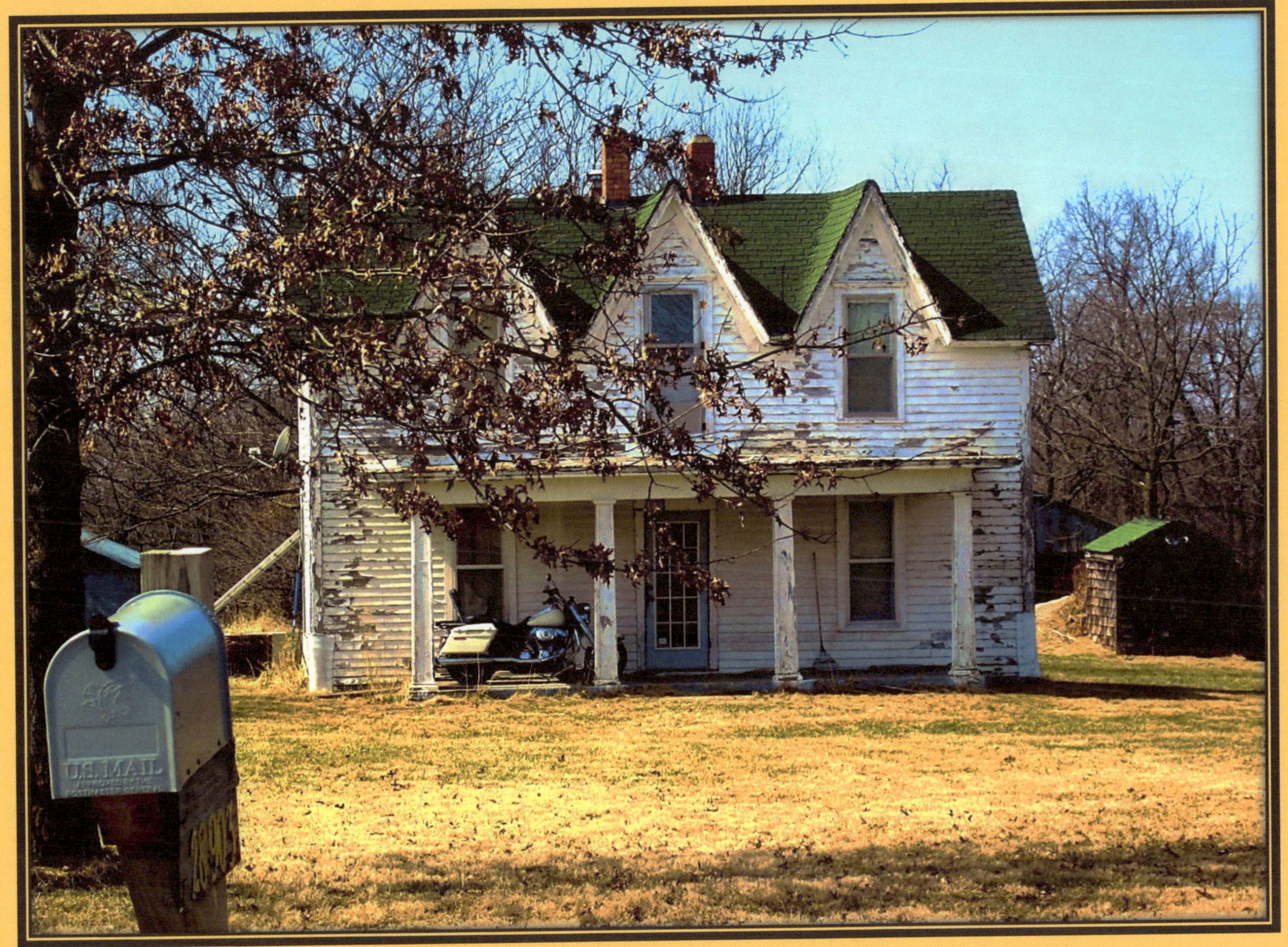

Rural Missouri in the fall is a comfortable place to be.

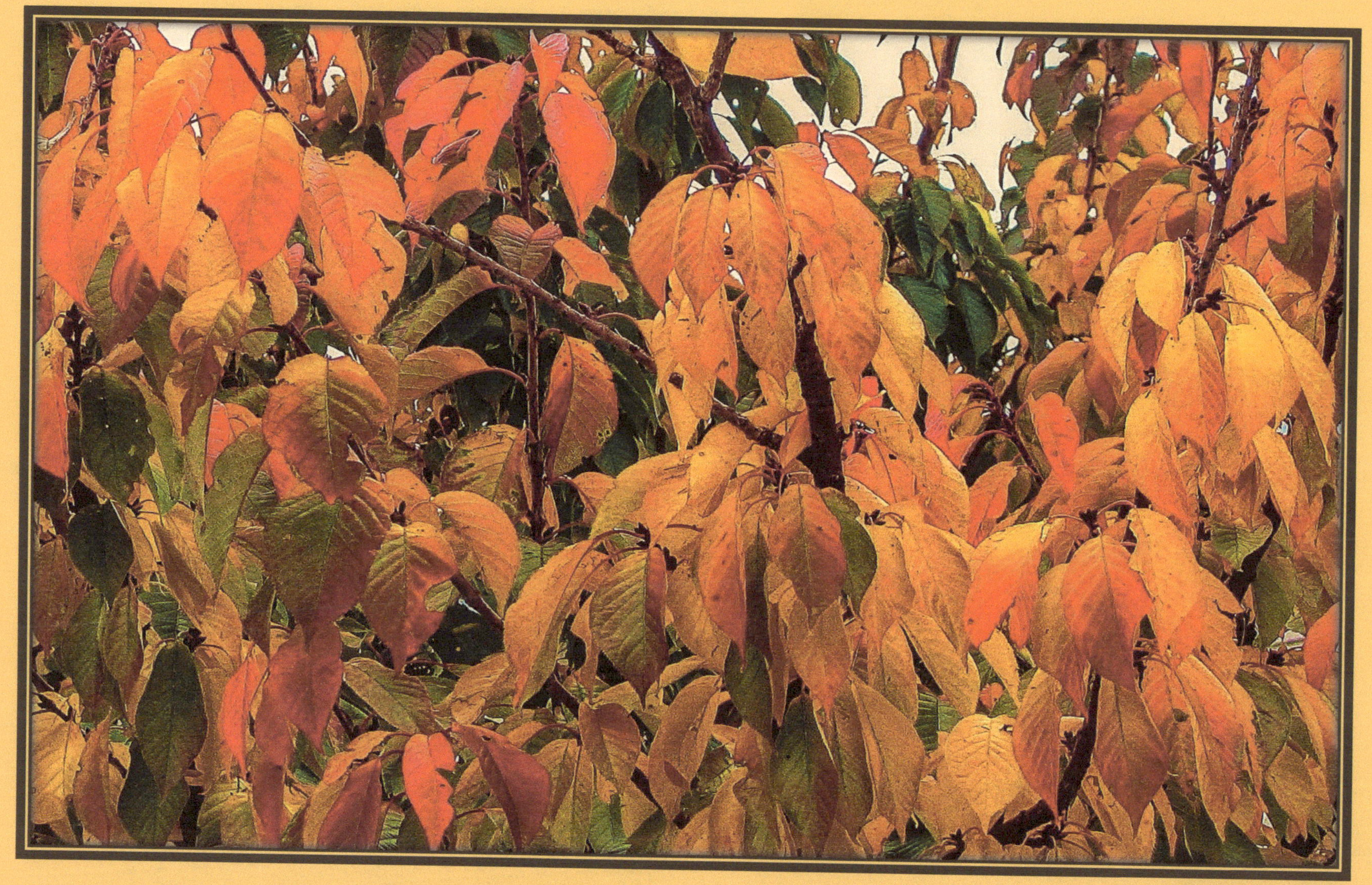

But soon, her fruitful plains will feel
the bite of frost.

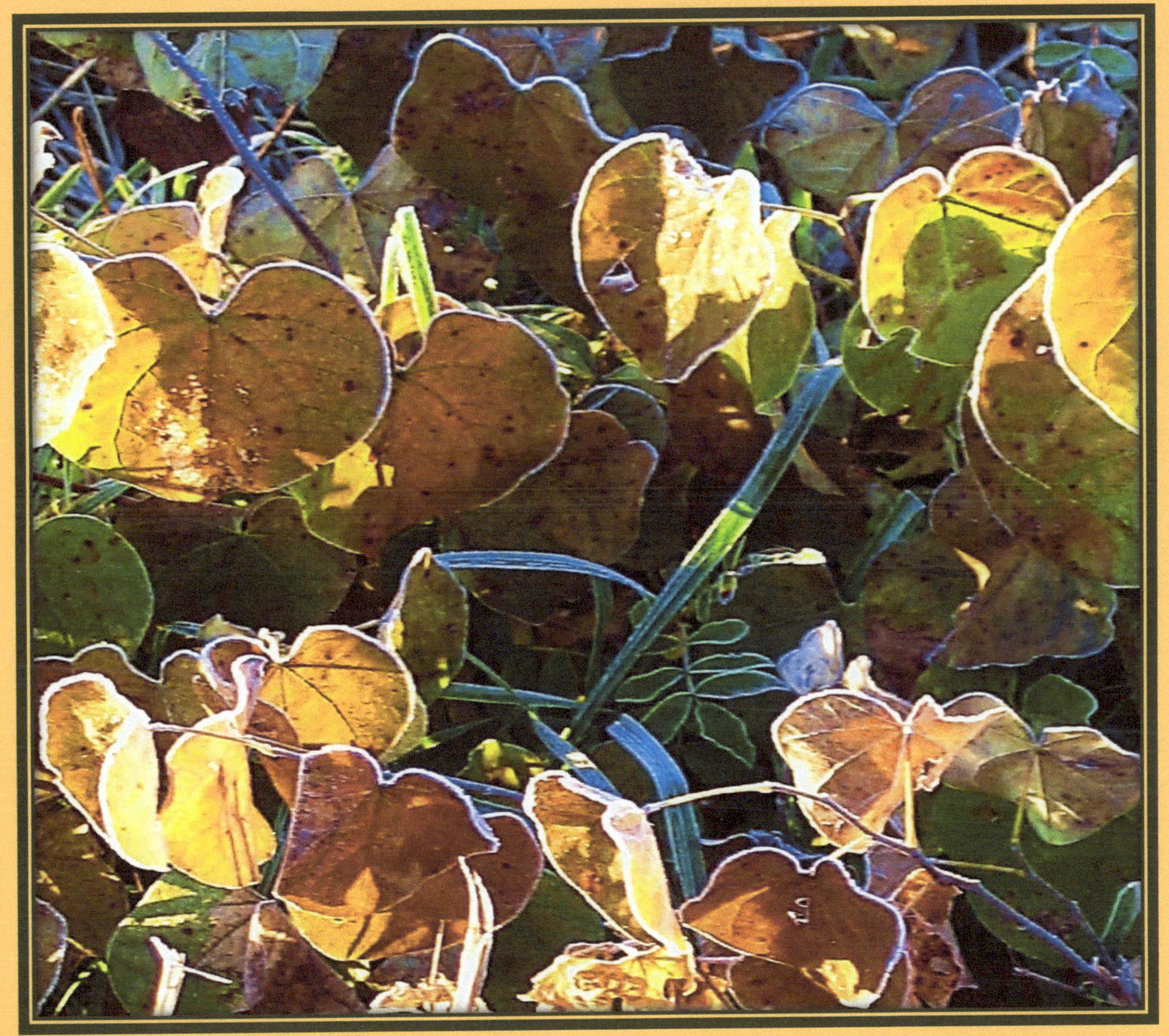

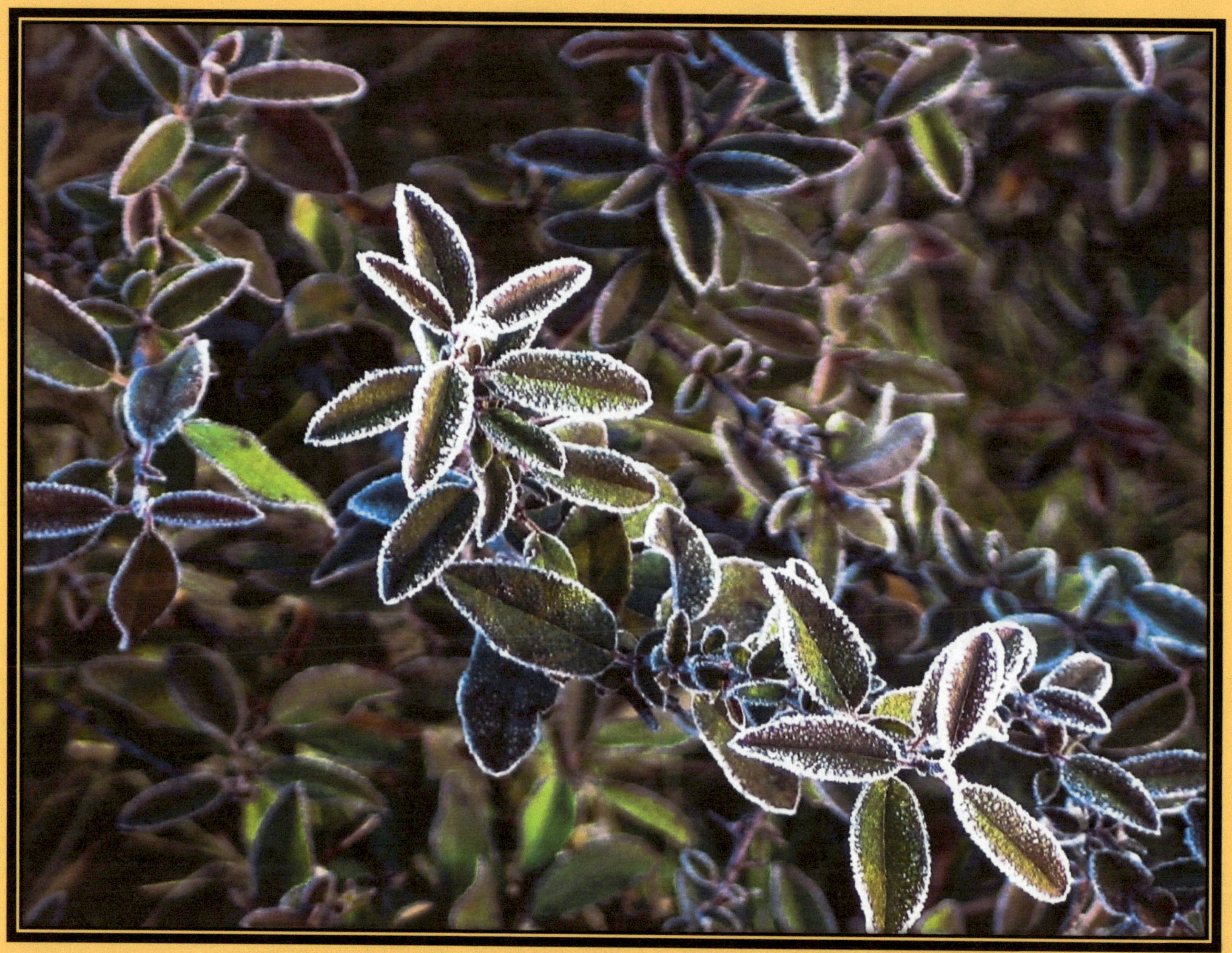

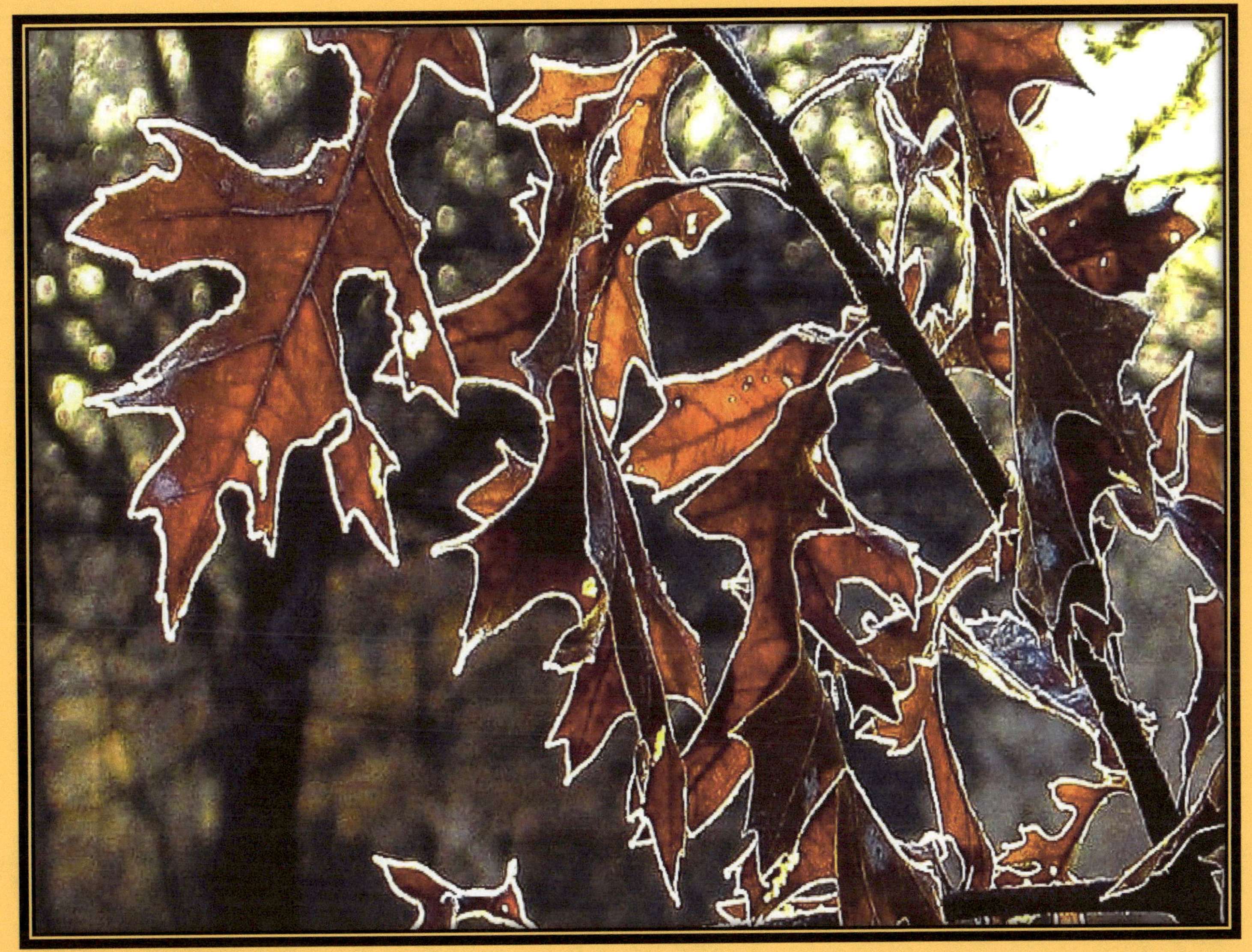

As all of life settles in for winter.

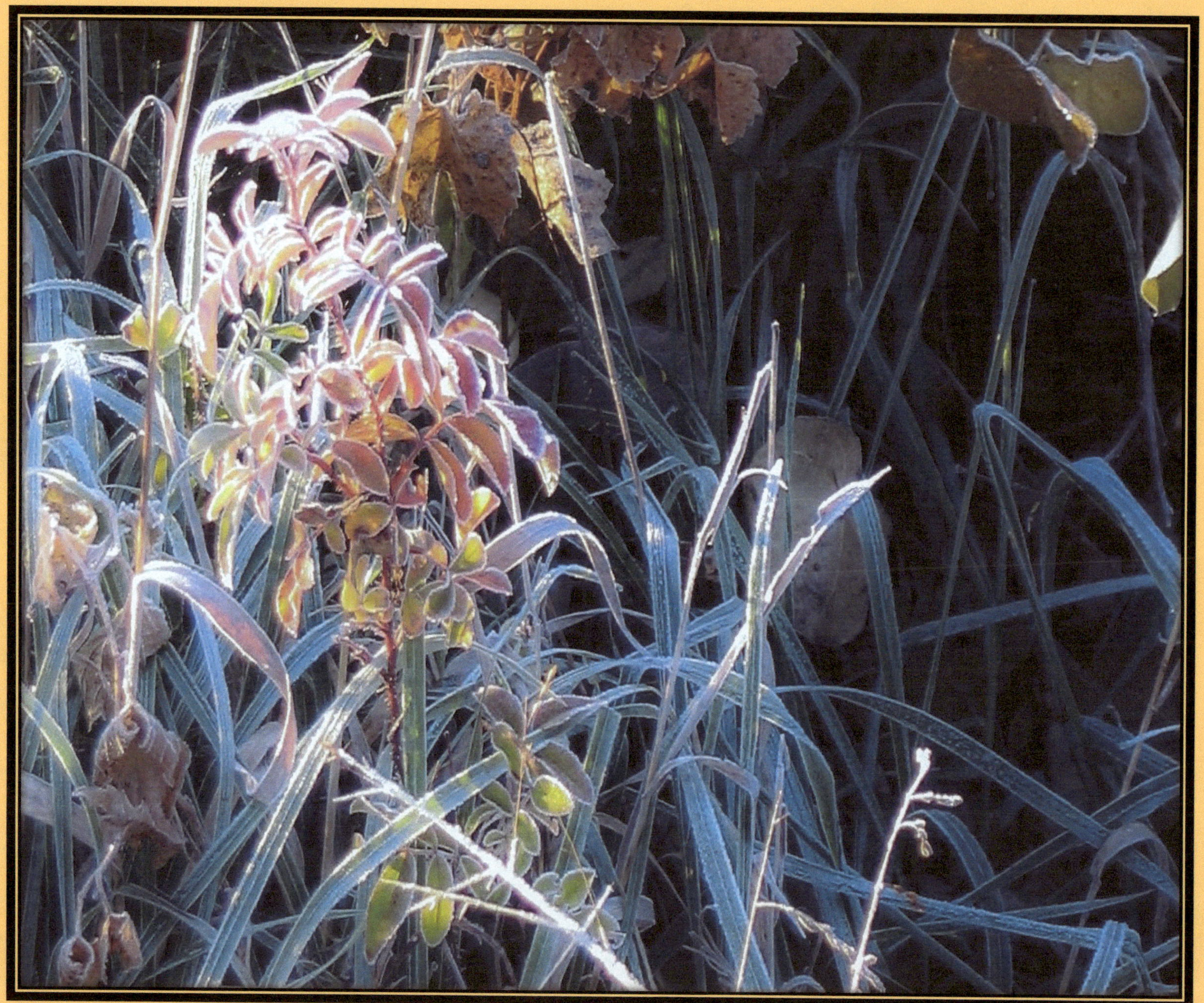